Taste the Purple

A Novel by Adam Mayer

*This book is dedicated to my wonderful wife
Christiana who has given me unconditional
love, has always supported me, puts up with
my madness, my world of insanity and has
always been there for me. And if I didn't
dedicate it to her, she would have killed me.*

ISBN: 978-1497456570

https://www.facebook.com/tastethepurple

Chapter One

John arrived at work and noticed that the front door of the office was burned. A giant letter E was spray painted on it in fluorescent orange. He thought to himself that this can't be good. The door was charred black and still warm. The paint on it was still wet. He walked in and saw Barbara sitting at the front desk. She smiled brightly at him as she did every morning.

"What happened to the door?" John nervously asked. He always got butterflies in his stomach whenever he talked to Barbara.

"It got burned" Barbara calmly responded.

"What's with the letter E?" John asked hoping that he could find out what it meant. Yet something deep down inside of him realized that he equally hoped to never know.

"I hear it's the calling card of the Brazilian Mafia," Barbara said without any concern or panic in her voice. Still smiling, she looked at John. She was as relaxed as someone lying in a hammock.

John was just about to question her about that but the phone rang. Barbara was the receptionist and the company dispatcher as well as the office manager. She was the den mom for the office, keeping everything running smoothly. No matter how crazy it got in there, it never fazed her. She was always calm, happy and never angry.

Barbara was the daughter of his boss, Henry Jenkins, the owner of the company. Henry was never around and when he was he could never remember the names of any of his employees. He started the company thirty years ago and due to his character many people didn't question his business practices. John was pretty sure it wasn't illegal, but couldn't say for sure if it was legal. He knew this was something he shouldn't be worrying about but it still gnawed away at him.

Barbara had just hung up the phone and before John could get a word out, the phone rang again. He thought to himself that whenever he tries to talk to her there is always something interfering, always something stopping him. He looked at her and thought she was the most beautiful woman he's ever known. She was smart, calm and collected. She had soft pale skin; medium length brunette hair and a Rubenesque figure that John thought made her look like a goddess. And she was quiet. She never spoke much but when she did it was always direct and important. He felt silly to have a childhood crush at his age.

John decided it wasn't worth getting himself stressed this early in the morning since that would come soon enough. John walked into the main office area where the technicians sat. His other co-workers were already there. William had been working there for two years now. He was a decent technician but seemed to have a lot of issues with his personal life and usually had to leave early or disappear for hours on end. And then there was Fred.

No one knew much about Fred, like his last name or where he lived. John had worked here for seven years and no matter how early he would arrive Fred was there. No matter how late he stayed, Fred would never leave. He didn't say much and when he did it was generally discomforting. He would constantly stare at John without saying anything. At first he thought it was his way of being friendly, but after time he realized that it just creeped him out. He avoided eye contact with Fred as much as possible and in general stayed away from him.

William looked up at John. "Hey buddy I need some

help. Someone set fire to my girlfriend's cat and I need to find her another one. Do you know someone I can steal a cat from?"

John looked at William with a look of confusion. "Did you see the front door?"

"Yeah, I hear it's the calling card of the Brazilian Mafia. So do you know where I can get a cat?"

"No, no I don't. Aren't you worried about the door? Why is the Mafia coming after us?"

William shrugged. "Probably one of old man Jenkins's botched deals. Look, if you can't help me get a cat I'm going to need for you to cover for me a few hours this morning."

John felt his stress rising. "I am not going to cover for you to go out and steal a cat. Do that on your own time."

"What about a goat? I know someone who has a goat."

"Don't you think your girlfriend would notice the difference between a cat and a goat?"

John sat down, logged into his computer just as their supervisor Tim walked into the room. Tim had no background in engineering or any technology for that matter. He would try and motivate the technicians, but it always failed. He would organize events for the workers to do after hours, but no one would attend. There were rumors that he didn't have a wife and that the photo on his desk was the one that came with the frame. John used to think that Tim was complex and misunderstood, but over time he realized that he was just an idiot.

"You guys see the game last night?" Tim asked looking around the room hoping for someone to acknowledge him.

William decided to play along, "What game would that be?"

Tim looked nervous, "I don't know. The game you know, the one that was on last night. Right?"

William looked at Tim with a devilish grin on his face. "No Tim, tell us all about it. What sport were they playing?"

One of William's favorite things was to torment Tim. He actually enjoyed making everyone's life miserable, but torturing Tim was his favorite. Mostly because he would walk into his traps. About a year earlier Tim bought a new dictionary which he showed off to the office. William told him that this was the new edition that removed the word gullible from the dictionary and Tim actually checked.

John decided he should try and save Tim. "Didn't see it. I was watching a movie last night."

"Which one?", Tim inquired.

"One of my favorites, the classic Grand Illusion by Jean Renoir. They were showing it on television last night, and it's one of those movies you just have to watch."

"Oh, I know. It's a great movie!" Tim responded with great pleasure.

"You've seen it?" John happily responded.

"No, no I've never seen it."

"Well you've hear of it then?"

"Nope, never heard of it. What was the name again?"

"What was the final score of the game Tim?" William chimed in, not willing to let Tim off the hook.

Tim had learned to ignore William, not by an active choice but more of a primal defense mechanism. He turned back to John. "John, did you ever get to that restaurant I told you about?"

John breathed a slight sigh. "Yes I did. It was closed by the Board of Health when I went over there."

"Okay then", Tim responded, "Say, any of you want

to come over this weekend for a barbecue at my place?"

John shook his head no. William, not wanting to miss an opportunity to torture Tim, quickly piped up. "I'd love to, but I've been looking forward so long to getting my root canal, and this weekend is the only time they can do it."

Tim didn't know if William was lying or being serious. He could never tell since William spoke with such serious honesty. "You can always stop by before or after the root canal, I'll have soft food."

"Oh, no can do. The root canal is going on all weekend. Maybe next time."

Tim looked confused but shrugged it off. "Well men, go out there today and make the company proud. It takes hard work to make it pay off. Think above the line. Working is payment to avoid the fees of laziness. You can't spell succeed without the letter d. If you avoid the hard path, the easy one will find its way back home to haunt your favorite practice. Remember that dedication to integrity is greater than the showcase of forgetting how to avoid the best practice of keeping pace with the advanced technology of the past. This is how Edison invented the Tesla Coil."

William looked at Tim square in the eye. "It was Nikola Tesla who invented the Tesla Coil. That's why they named it the Tesla Coil, they named it after him. Otherwise it would be known as the Edison Coil."

Tim shifted his eyes back and forth and looked scared. "Yeah, but still."

John turned away, he had enough of this. He was still upset about the front door. He thought to himself this is why I keep having nightmares. As soon as he turned in his chair he saw Fred staring at him. He was holding a plastic bag and was chewing on it. John noticed that Fred would eat strange things; a few weeks ago he was convinced that Fred was eating a cookie smothered with mayonnaise. John figured that Fred worked with old man Jenkins when they started the company but he never knew. Once he asked Fred when did he start working here, how did he learn his trade, where does he live? Fred just stared at him and then tossed a handful of paper clips into his mouth and started chewing on them.

Fred was clearly the most knowledgeable employee who worked there. He knew every piece of equipment backwards and forwards and could rebuild any of it blindfolded. He was ignored by everyone, like the way you would ignore a tree or rock on the ground. At times John wondered if he was real or some sort of Tyler Durden that his mind made up. This much he knew, he avoided working with him unless he had no choice.

"Oh, and John, John?" John turned back and saw that Tim was talking to him again. "John, I'm going to need you to head over to the Wilkinson's factory this morning. They called in a repair last night."

John froze for a moment. "Not the Wilkinson place. That's out in the dead zone."

"Stop it", Tim responded. "That's just a name; it's not a death zone. Better take someone with you, that's a really old unit out there."

"Can't do it, got to get ready for my root canal." William responded.

"Right," Tim acknowledged. He looked at John, "Better get going, the early frog avoids the flaming hail."

John realized that there was no way out of this job. He looked at Fred who finally was no longer staring at him; he was staring at the empty wall. "Okay Fred, let's go. Fred? Fred?"

...

A short while later John was driving north on highway 29. He looked out his window and saw piles of bones and dead animal carcasses spewed all along the side of the road. Nothing was growing, no grass, no trees, just a eerie weird gray color across the landscape. He thought that there was less life out here than on the moon. He wondered if the rumors of this being a illegal nuclear disposal area was not just an urban legend.

John frustrated proclaimed, "I thought Tim said that this wasn't a death zone, that it was just a name."

Fred staring out the window blankly calmly responded "What he meant was that this is unincorporated land and that there is no zoning out here."

...

A few hours later John walked back into the office, his eyes and throat burning. He was angry and frustrated. He was going to take it out on Tim. He looked in Tim's office and he wasn't there. He walked over to Barbara and was going to ask her where is Tim. But before he could speak the phone rang and Barbara smiled and held up her finger to let him know to wait a moment. John sat down on the lobby couch and looked out the window. Across the street a garbage dumpster was on fire outside the back of the dry cleaner's store. Two men were unsuccessfully trying to put out the fire by throwing water at it. John heard a fire engine in the distant background getting louder.

Chapter Two

John was sitting at a folding table and looking around him. He was in an open field full of grass; the table was right in the middle of nowhere. He was holding a soldering iron and as he looked down and pointed the iron he noticed that in front of him was a plate with a piece of birthday cake. He felt confused and when he looked up he was now at a bus stop wearing slippers and his night clothing, sweatpants and a tee shirt. Next to him was a cactus that was playing ranchera music. Someone dressed up in a Victorian era suit walked up to him.

"The bus is in the stratosphere so it will take time for the chicken to burn the gold," the man said to John.

All of a sudden a bus pulled up and John's grandfather walked off the bus. He was dressed in a black suit and was smoking a cigar.

"Grandpa Albert, what are you doing here?"

"John, my boy. Come to your grandfather."

John was now dressed in a green sweater, the one his grandmother gave him for Christmas when he was ten. It was an ugly lime green sweater that he hated, but his mom told him that he needed to wear it to show respect. He was now in his grandparents' home and walked over to his grandfather who was sitting in his favorite chair.

"Grandpa, I miss you so much. I was so sad at your funeral. I love you, grandpa."

"I know my boy, I love you too. But I must tell you something important. I must tell you about Henderson's Floor Wax."

"But grandpa, why do I need to know about floor wax?"

"Don't argue with me! Henderson's makes the best floor wax out there and it's on sale this week at

Calvin's supermarket. Only $2.99 a bottle, you should get a case."

"Grandpa, I don't have wood floors, my apartment is all carpet. I can't use floor wax."

"Nonsense! Everyone needs floor wax."

John looked around and he was now in his apartment living room. His grandfather was standing in the middle. He opened the bottle of floor wax and started to squeeze the wax onto his carpet.

"You see me boy, how well it works. Only Henderson's Floor Wax will get your floor clean. You want clean floors don't you? Well, don't you, John?"

"Yes, grandpa, I want clean floors. I'll buy Harper's Floor Wax today."

"It's Henderson's. Listen to me, Henderson's Floor Wax. Buy it this week on sale at Calvin's supermarket."

John opened his eyes and looked at the ceiling. Dreams like this had been happening more often than he wanted them. They bothered him, but more than that, it frustrated him when he would go to the supermarket. He dreamed that his great aunt told him to buy shoe polish and he got eight cans. What really gets him is that he doesn't even own a pair of shoes that they could be used on. He looked over at the clock and the bright display showed 2:19. He realized that he won't be getting back to sleep anytime soon, might as well check his email.

John noticed a message that had just showed up about an hour ago from his best friend Joseph. It was another one of his poems. John had been friends with Joseph for twenty five years and at some point in high school Joseph started to write abstract poetry. He would show them to John to get his opinion of them. John didn't understand them, occasionally found them funny, but most of the time was very confused. This new one was about Joseph's frustration with a local fast food restaurants commercial campaign. He was angry that the commercials for Hamburger Prince were subliminal and that the children they used in the commercial were really elves. John knew he was not literal about the elves, but he sometimes wondered if Joseph had trouble defining the lines of reality.

Either way Joseph had been his closest friend, pretty much his brother. They were both in second grade when they met and were like peas in a pod. Although physically they were as far apart as two people could be. John had light blond hair as a kid that got darker as he got older, Joseph's hair was always jet black. John was a chubby kid, not obese but husky while Joseph was skinny as a rail. Kids would make fun of them and call them ten since when they stood next to each other they would form a one and a zero. By high school John turned towards computers to escape the abuse. Joseph started writing poetry. His poems were like nightmares, full of frustrations and very angry. John was confused since Joseph's parents were the nicest people you could ever know. After John's parents passed away when he was in college they adopted him as their other son. To this day every year for Thanksgiving and Christmas he spends them with Joseph's family.

At the bottom of the email Joseph invited him to his next recital at the Cafe Wombat in one week. Joseph would perform there on a regular basis but this is the first time he was the headliner. Back in college he would go to open mic poetry night. John would go down for the cheap food and beer and to support his friend. John never enjoyed poetry much but it seemed to have a bigger following that he thought.

John thought back to those days in college, when he didn't have nightmares. When he could still get a good night's sleep. He wasn't too fond of engineering school, pure brainwashing in his opinion, but he could clear his mind at night and fall asleep. He realized that the nightmares probably started when he was 19 and heard the news that his mother died. She was in her fifties and died of a heart attack one day out of nowhere. Her health had been fine and then all of a sudden she died. At the funeral he saw how upset his father was, something about that bothered him. His father was always emotionless, a stone face no matter what. John realized that one of the difficulties of growing up is finding out that your parents are people too. A few months later his father died from a heart attack as well giving John a great deal of panic that he too will fall victim to the same ailment one day very soon. The problem was that now the nightmares were happening more often and when they weren't nightmares, they were the strangest dreams you could imagine. He never told Joseph about them, but then wondered if he could use them in his poems.

John decided that he should at least attempt to try and get a little bit more sleep. He knew if he tried to watch a movie he would get caught up and never get to bed. It was a debate between staying up watching television or lying in bed and staring at the ceiling. He did a mental coin flip and decided on bed. As he walked back into his bedroom he looked out his apartment window and noticed that down the street on the sidewalk there was a fire burning. Someone had set fire to a pile of clothing. It burned bright; lighting up the entire street like it was a bright sunny day. Someone came running out of the front door of the apartment building with a fire extinguisher and frantically tried to put out the fire.

Chapter Three

"And the librarian said, 'If that's the potato salad, then what I did I put on the bookcase!'"

Tim looked around the office and saw that not only was no one laughing but no one seemed to be paying attention. "John, didn't you find that funny?"

John sat staring blankly into his laptop not noticing that Tim was talking until he mentioned his name. He figured he should answer him to speed up the process of getting him back to his office and ultimately leaving him alone. "I'm sorry, Tim. What was that?"

"Didn't you find that funny", Tim answered again.

"Um, yes, very funny. Your best one yet," John answered sarcastically.

"Like that one, William?" Tim not being able to read John's sarcasm and now thinking he could get William to join in was wading in dangerous water.

William looked at Tim, smiling and nodding his head up and down. "No."

Tim lost the smile on his face and became more serious, looking directly at William. "I need to talk to you about something that is becoming an issue. You have to stop faking your death at customer sites. The last customer was so upset that she had to be taken to the hospital for chest pains."

"I can't help that," William responded defensively. "I had no choice. She had me checking her electrical outlets. That's not my job, I'm not an electrician. It was the only way for me to leave that location."

Tim shook his head. "No, that is not the only option. Look, we have to pay for the ambulance ride. Do you know how expensive those are?"

"No I don't, but I will say they are very comfortable. And the last EMT was a really cute redhead. I think she was into me."

"That's the point, Tim responded to William. "We are not only paying for the customer's ride but yours as well. This has to stop. Now I want you to promise me that you won't do this again."

William got a devilish smile on his face. "Tim, if oranges were blue, would they still be called oranges?"

Tim looked very confused. "What does that have to do with this?"

"Everything" William confidently responded. "And I think that clears up the problem."

Tim wasn't sure exactly what happened but decided in order to cut his losses he should walk away with a possible tie. He knew that he wasn't going to win over William. He stood there for almost a minute not saying anything and then turned and walked back to his office.

"Well played, good man," John said to William. "Well played indeed." John looked closely at William's face and couldn't stop staring.

"What's wrong? Why are you staring at me?"

John thought for a second and then decided he had to say something. "Can I ask you a personal question?"

"Sure, go ahead."

"What's up with your face?" William's face was full of scratch marks. "Were you trying to claw your eyes out or something?"

William laughed. "It's from my girlfriend's new cat. It attacked me last night."

"This is the same one you cut out yesterday to steal?"

"No, someone ended up setting that one on fire. This is another one I found last night. Don't think it likes me. Can only hope it finds the same fate as the others."

"Well, one of them looks really infected. I mean real bad. You should take care of that, maybe see a doctor." William shrugged and then went back to looking at his computer.

At this point John realized that he would need more coffee in order to try and survive the day. He walked over to the break room where he found Fred sitting there looking at a television set. The set was on a station of static; Fred sat attentively staring at it like it was a regular program. John found himself staring at the TV for a moment before he stopped himself and thought, "What am I doing?"

...

"So here's the equipment room, the box is over there." The customer led John into a cramped closet that would have trouble fitting a few coats into. "Think you can fix it?"

"How long has it been out of service?" John asked.

"I don't know, about a week I guess?"

John grabbed a screwdriver and opened up the device. He looked down into it and couldn't believe his eyes. He stared for a few seconds that felt like hours in his mind. "Well, sir, I think I've found your problem. You may want to come over here and see this for yourself."

The customer looked into the opened device. "Is that what I think it is?"

"Yes, sir," John said calmly "Your device is full of eels." Inside the device was about twelve small eels that were wriggling around. "My guess is that this is causing the device not to work. They must have chewed through the power supply and looks like most of the circuit boards as well."

"Well, I didn't do it" the customer responded

defensively.

"Sir, I know you had nothing to do with this."

"How did they get in there?"

John shrugged. "I don't know. I have another unit in my van. I will go get it and replace this one."

"What's going to happen to the eels?"

"I don't know. Guess I'll get rid of them for you."

"Do they belong to Jenkins Electrical?"

"What?"

"Do they belong to your company? They were inside the equipment."

John thought for a moment. "No sir, they don't belong to Jenkins Electrical."

"So then I can have them?"

John was confused. For a moment he started to think that he was having a dream, that it was still last night and he finally fell asleep. That though faded quickly as John realized that this is not as strange as his dreams so it must be happening. "Yes, sir, you can have them if you want."

The customer's face lit up like a kid in a candy store and he reached in and grabbed the eels. John turned away and walked out of the customer site and down the sidewalk to his van. He realized that he was parked on a hill and he was going to have carry the device back up the hill, something he was not looking forward to. John opened the side door of his van and it slammed shut as soon as he let go of the door. He realized that he was going to have to prop the door open. He grabbed a screwdriver and wedged it in the side of the door and climbed inside the back of his van. He looked for a replacement device and found one buried under a bunch of other boxes. As he was pulling them off, John accidentally bumped the screwdriver and the door slammed shut.

"Great", John sighed. As he pulled the lever to open

the door again it wouldn't open. He pulled hard and it didn't budge. John wasn't claustrophobic, but the last place he wanted to be was trapped inside a van. He kept thinking to himself, why is this door locked? Why is it not opening? What am I doing wrong? John took a breath to calm down and think logically. He realized that there had to be a simple solution to this problem. At that moment he looked at the side window and saw the disclaimer for child proof locks.

He said out loud "Why would you put child proof locks on a work vehicle? Who would be so stupid as to set the child proof --" John stopped himself and realized who set the child proof lock. "I am going to kill William when I get back to the office."

Over the past two years John and William would play pranks on one another. The first one John remembered is when he asked William to get something from his van and gave him the keys. The next time John started the vehicle he found out that William turned on the heat to full blast, radio was full volume on static, windshield wipers going, turn blinkers, pretty much everything that could be turned on was done.

To get him back John got William's phone and set the language to Portuguese. William then removed John's email account off the server. John put bubble wrap under William's tires. William filled a box of confetti over John's desk that John accidentally triggered when he reached up for a manual. But there was one that stood above them all, the Sergeant Peppers of all pranks.

William made up a crude sign that he left on his desk with the initials STFU, the abbreviation for shut the f**k up. He would hold it up when he didn't want anyone to bother him. One day John printed out "I'm Gay" and taped it over the front of the sign and placed it back face down the way William would always keep it. One day after that Tim was trying to get everyone in the office to come to the conference room for a meeting. William wouldn't move from his desk. Tim was standing with the entire office looking at William as he held up the sign without looking at it first. There was incredible laughter from everyone. William was annoyed and demanded to know who messed with his sign. When John finally caught his breath he told him that he had been waiting for over three months for him to pick up that sign.

John knew it was only a matter of time before William got him back. John realized that if you live by the sword you die by the sword. It had been almost six months since that prank John remembered, he didn't know how long ago William had placed this time bomb prank on him. John wasn't angry, just aggravated that on a day after he got practically no sleep, this was the day he would face this prank.

John realized that in order to get out of the van someone would have to open the door for him. He didn't want to call William that would be admitting defeat. Nor could he let anyone else in the office know because it would get back to William. If he could get the door to be opened, he could fix the child proof lock and no one would know that he got caught.

John looked out the window to see if anyone was on the street that he could signal over to let him out. There were people walking past him but no one noticed him. John started to bang on the window and signal to come towards the van. Finally one man wearing a brown hat stopped but just stood there looking at John.

John shouted, "Please open the door!" but it was muffled. The man stood there like he was watching a television in a store window. A few more people started to gather around and watch John. John became more animated and started tapping the window and made the motion of opening the door.

A woman in the crowd asked out loud "What is he doing?"

The man in the brown hat said, "I think he's some sort of street performer."

Another man observing wearing a green coat chimed in, "He's not very good. What is he trying to do?"

A woman watching with her child also joined the conversation "I think he's one of those people who act out things that are not there, like walking in the wind and stuff."

"A clown," the man in the green coat responded.

"No," said the man in the brown hat, "You mean a mime."

The first woman responded "I though mimes were silent. I think I heard him just say something."

John shouted "Yes, please let me out." Again it was muffled so the crowd didn't understand what he said.

"You see," the woman said while pointing at John. "He spoke. That's not a mime."

"Or a really bad one," the man in the green coat added.

"Hey, you remember that classic movie about mimes?" the man in the brown hat asked the crowd.

John shouted from inside the van, "You're talking about *Children of Paradise*."

The man in the brown hat looked at John, "What?"

John looked around and found a notepad, wrote *Children of Paradise* on the page and held it up to the window. The man in the brown hat shook his head, "No, that's not it"

The man in the green coat eyes light up. "I know, you mean *It*."

18

"Yes, exactly. Thank you, it was *It*." The man in the brown hat happily replied.

John banged on the window and wrote on another page on the notepad that It was about a clown and held it up to the window. Everyone in the crowd was disappointed.

The woman with the child spoke up, "Oh, I know, *Killer Klowns From Outer Space.*"

John smacked his forehead in frustration and quickly wrote on the notepad that it has clowns in the title so it can't be a movie about mimes and held it up to the window. A few people in the crowd responded with agreement.

The man in the brown hat spoke again. "Either way I don't like mimes, they support the metric system." A few gasps came from the crowd. "It's true. I've seen them publicly announce it."

"If they're mimes, how did they announce it? They can't speak?" the woman responded.

John banged on the glass and held up the notepad saying that a mute can't speak, mimes perform without speaking. The man in the brown hat added his agreement, "The mime is right, they can speak." He paused for a moment to think. "But they do yell when you punch them. No, the mime didn't tell me. It was on a flyer talking about it and how they plan to protest the anti-metric system rally next week."

John banged on the window again and wrote, "I am not a mime."

"He says he's not a mime," replied the man in the brown hat, "but I still don't like them. How can they support the metric system?" A wave of agreement came from the crowd.

The woman proudly announced, "See I knew he wasn't a mime. He was talking during his act."

John was getting stressed and aggravated. He was

thinking his best bet would have been to sit in the back and wait for a junkie to break into the van and steal his copper wire. At least then he could make an escape. He smacked his forehead again and realized what an idiot he is. He wrote on the notepad and held it up to the window saying please let me out I am locked inside the van - child proof lock is set.

The woman said, "I see, he's making a political statement. He's saying he is trapped by society, in this case his van, and he wants to break out of his shell and become his own man by joining the crowd."

The crowd watching this was now at least thirty people. A much older man piped up, "How can he become an individual by joining the crowd? Isn't he more of an individual by staying locked inside his van?"

The woman responded, "I see your point, but maybe there is a much more complex reason why he is trapped inside the van. Maybe there's something more to it than just being locked inside of a van."

John yelled, "No, I'm locked in! Please let me out!" Again his yelling was muffled and no one understood him.

"Well, I'll give him credit for his originality," said the man with the brown hat. "He's not that bad as a street performer. And he looks like someone who also hates mimes." At that moment he pulled a coin from his pocket and tossed it at the window of the van. Additional people started to throw coins at John. John started to bang his head repeatedly on the window out of frustration, which drew great applause from the crowd. Just when he though it couldn't get worse he noticed that his supervisor Tim was in the crowd watching this. John quickly moved to the back of the van hoping that he didn't see him.

"Where did he go?" the woman with the child asked.

"He must be getting ready for the next show," responded the old man.

Tim walked towards the van. "John, are you in there?" he asked.

"Please open the door."

"I couldn't hear you. What was that?"

John sat with his back against the wall of the van looking out the window at Tim. He made a hand gesture signaling for Tim to come in.

Tim opened the door and said, "I couldn't hear --" and the door slammed shut. He opened it again. "I said I couldn't --" again the door slammed shut. On the third attempt John leapt forward and nearly knocking Tim over and stepped out of the van. He immediately set the child proof latch to not lock on him again. As he turned around the crowd was still watching him and started to applaud again. The small child with the woman ran up and threw a handful of pennies at John.

"You know you're not allowed to accept tips while you are on the job," Tim said to John.

"I'm not collecting tips," John fired back angrily.

"Look, I'm just saying I have no problem with you being artistic and all, but you do have a job to do. Although it is nice to see your creative side. But you can't leave your money here on the street."

"It's not my money. I am not an artist. I got locked inside my van. That's it. I came out of the building there to get a replacement unit, and got locked inside my van."

"So you're going to leave the money here?"

"Sure, let some homeless guy pick it up."

"No problem. Don't worry about it. Say you want to join me for some lunch?"

"No, Tim, I don't want to eat lunch. I'm on a job right now."

"You don't like lunch? You know it's the most important meal of the day."

"No, Tim, that's breakfast. Breakfast is the most important meal of the day. Look, forget meals. We got a bigger problem here. I have to replace this unit," John opened the van door reached in and pulled out a large box, "because the one inside that office building is full of eels."

"Eels you say. What kind of eels?"

"I don't know, I'm not a reptile specialist"

"Wonder what a reptile specialist is called?"

"I don't know, Tim, I just don't know."

"I'll look it up on my phone."

"It doesn't matter."

"Here we go. A reptile specialist is a herpetologist."

"That's great."

"Hmm, doesn't list eels though. Oh, here we go. Eels are not reptiles, they are an elongated fish. Are you sure those were eels?"

"I don't know, maybe they were snakes."

"Well there is a big difference between an eel and a snake you know."

"No, I don't know. All I know is that when I open a piece of equipment, I don't expect to see a bunch of creatures moving around in there eating the circuit boards. Where is this stuff from? I think you're going to have to talk to Mr. Jenkins about this. This can be a real big problem if there are others like these out there."

Tim thought for a moment. "All right, why don't you stop by my office when you get back in to the shop."

John felt a little bit relieved. "Thank you. I will stop in later." John picked up the box and walked back to the office. He looked behind him and noticed that Tim was looking around to see if anyone was looking at him and then proceeded to start picking up the change tossed at the van. John turned back and just before he walked back into the office building noticed down the street a brick wall with a faded letter E in fluorescent orange paint on it.

Chapter Four

John arrived back at the office. He walked in and saw Barbara hanging up the phone. John stopped for a second to look at her. He realized that she had never looked so beautiful and he wanted her to know it.

"Is Tim in his office?" John asked, not having the courage to say what he wanted to say. Barbara shook her head and smiled. John got those butterflies in his stomach again. He thought to himself I need to get over this. "Barbara, I want to say something." She looked at him, her eyes smiling brightly, a soft smile on her face, looking attentively at John. "I want to tell you--." All of a sudden the phone rang; Barbara gave a slight shrug and answered the phone. John stood there frustrated for a moment and then walked over to the break room to get himself another cup of coffee. As he walked out and turned the corner he ran into Fred standing in the middle of the hallway. Fred was just standing there motionless. John looked at him, not sure if he was a zombie or in a trance. He waved his hand in front of Fred's eyes and he did not blink. John carefully walked around Fred who did not move. He went to his desk, sat down and leaned his head back and stared at the ceiling thinking when will this day end.

Albert walked into the technician area. "Great news everybody. I have tickets to my new movie," he proudly announced. "I know you all want to go."

Albert was the company bookkeeper and handled payroll. He was a young man who was studying to become a CPA. In his spare time he would make bizarre avant-garde underground independent films. He dreamed of becoming an unknown, unappreciated underground director like Kenneth Anger.

William looked up from his computer. "I would rather be trapped in a burning building."

"John, I know you want to go. You enjoy movies. You're the only person I know who has seen *Big Deal on Madonna Stree*t more times than I have," Albert proclaimed.

John shrugged, "Well, I have seen it twice. So what's the movie about?"

"It's called *The Agony of the Tooth.* It's a story about a man who has a horrible toothache and how he is trying to find parking at the dentist's office but can't find any."

"So, it's a short film then?" William asked.

"Well, part one is three hours and twenty five minutes," Albert responded.

"I take it back; I'd rather light myself on fire and then run into a burning building." William suddenly got that devilish look back on his face. "What about your last film, when is that going to be shown?"

Albert looked visibly annoyed. "I don't know. It's up to the United Way if they will allow the footage to be released." Six months ago Albert was asked by the United Way to film a documentary about retired football players helping out at a nursing home. Instead he put together a football game between the retirees and the players.

"So what was the death toll?" William sarcastically asked.

"No one died." Albert thought for a moment, "but there were six broken hips and one heart attack. You would think retired football players would go half speed and not blindside tackle an eighty-five year old woman. I guess that's why they say if you go half speed you get hurt."

"Guess you never studied physics," William quipped. "It's much safer to get into a car accident at seventy miles an hour than going at fifteen."

Albert decided to ignore William. "John, you got to come, I got tickets for you."

"When is it?"

"It's tonight."

"I can't. I didn't get any sleep last night, I'm exhausted. Maybe I'll go see part two."

"No excuse. It's being hosted by the Philolaus Society during their monthly Christmas party. Here are two tickets, bring someone with you."

John looked at the tickets in Albert's hand and thought hard for a moment. He then grabbed them and looked more closely at them. "Seven thirty at the Antichthon Building on Maple Street. I have never seen that building before?"

"It's on the other side of the planetarium, but you can't see it from there, the Helios building keeps it hidden. Just look for me I'll be greeting people outside."

John took the tickets and put them in his pocket. He saw Tim walk by and head to his office. John realized he'd better talk to Tim and get it over with. He knocked on the door jamb of Tim's office, "Can I come in?"

Tim was caught off guard and quickly grabbed a bunch of papers on his desk and clumsily stuffed them into a desk drawer. "Yes please, come on in. What's up?"

"You told me to stop by your office when I got back."

"And you have. That's great. What's on your mind? Want to talk about movies?"

"No, Tim, I'm here to talk about the eels in the equipment. Remember earlier today?"

"Right, right, of course, the eels. So where are they?"

"Where are what?"

"The eels, where are they?"

"They're at the customer location. He wanted them."

"Why would you leave them there? That's company property."

"Since when did we start selling eels?"

"Anything that is in our equipment is company property. You don't have the right to give away company property. We'll just have to bill the customer for the eels."

"You think that's a smart idea? What is the price for a dozen eels? What if the customer doesn't pay?"

"Then we will have to deduct it from your pay."

"You can't do that," John said, deciding to call Tim's bluff.

Tim looked nervous. He wasn't expecting John to challenge him. William, that was to be expected even if he asked him what time it was, but not from John. Tim was thinking of how to respond. "Then we will take it from your bonus."

John got a smirk on his face. "What bonus? We don't get bonuses here. Or are you talking about my eel bonus?"

"Um," Tim paused for a few seconds realizing that he had no response. He weakly answered, "Yes."

John laughed, stood up and turned to walk out of Tim's office. Just before he walked out he turned back to Tim, "You just do that."

Outside of Tim's office John pulled the tickets out of his pocket. He stood there looking at the tickets. Then he thought about everything that had happened today, dealing with Tim and what a rotten day it had been. Suddenly he got an adrenaline rush and a thought popped into his head, I'm going to ask Barbara to go with me to the movie. A wave of panic came over him; he started to feel pins and needles in his legs. He felt flushed and dizzy. He closed his eyes, took a deep breath and then started walking. He felt like he was walking in a tunnel. He noticed nothing around him. He walked past Fred staring at him. Tim was walking out of his office and started to talk to John, but John didn't hear him. All he saw was Barbara sitting at her desk and he walked up to her. As soon as he opened his mouth the phone rang. John realized that it wasn't him holding him back; the phone was always ringing when he wanted to talk to Barbara. He gently took the receiver from Barbara's hand and hung up the phone. She looked up at him with a quizzical but admiring look.

"I have two tickets for Albert's movie tonight and I want you to be my date."

Barbara smiled brightly. "Yes." John was ready to argue his point to convince her to go out with him. Then he realized that she agreed. Now he really began to panic. He didn't think or plan this out; this was a spontaneous action, something that he would never do. And as a result didn't know what to do next and was visibly flustered. He attempted to speak.

"Yes. Great. Um, when should I get to pick up where I can take you time place." John realized he was babbling.

"Pick me up at six. You can take me out to dinner."

John felt his heart pounding. He looked Barbara in the eyes and noticed how blue they were. So calming, so soothing, he started to feel calmer by the second. Then he realized he had no idea where to take her out to. He didn't want to ask her where to go, he was afraid that she wouldn't think he was in control, especially after he made his dramatic move by pulling the phone out of her hands and asking her out.

Albert popped his head over the cubicle wall behind Barbara, obviously hearing the entire exchange. "I know the greatest restaurant that just opened up down the street from the event, Olaf's Thai. It's a new fusion Norwegian Thai restaurant. Try the herring Pad Thai, it's amazing."

John thought to himself, thank god. "Perfect, I'll pick you up at six." John turned and walked back into the technicians' area. He turned and walked back to Barbara's desk. "Where am I picking you up?"

Barbara smiled at John. "I've already texted it to you."

....

When John drove up to Barbara's apartment building, she was already waiting for him. He noticed that she had changed from her work clothes to a nice silk button down shirt with a pair of jeans. John thought that maybe he should have changed from his work clothes before the date, but too late now. As she walked towards his car he imagined her walking in a wedding gown down the aisle. She knocked on the passenger side window which shook John from his daydream. He stared blankly at her, she smiled back at him. He then realized that the door was locked and unlocked it for her.

"You look beautiful." John looked at Barbara and noticed that she was wearing makeup, something that she didn't do at work. But she was wearing so little you could barely tell. He thought she was beautiful without makeup but just the slightest bit made her look even more ravishing. John attempted to turn back into traffic, but he noticed that he was still in park. "Right, got to put the car into drive." Barbara giggled.

The outside of the restaurant looked like a pawn shop that someone abandoned years ago. There was a hand written sign taped to the inside window that said Olaf's Thai Restaurant and another crooked one below it that said open. The outside of the door had a sign that said push when it clearly was a door that needed to be pulled open. John opened the door and held it for Barbara. The inside of the restaurant was bleak; all the walls were painted white with no pictures on them. There was a statue of a Viking with a necklace made out of durian fruit around its neck. In the lobby there was a dead tree leaning against the wall. On the overhead speakers let out loud heavy metal music that was very fast with distorted guitars and shrieking. A waiter approached them. He was wearing a bright yellow sarong and a Viking helmet with horns.

"How many, please?"

John looked over his shoulder to see if there was anyone else who came in behind him, no one had. He then looked back at the waiter "Two for dinner, please." The waiter walked them to a small table inside the restaurant. There were about twelve tables; the only other patrons were a group of mimes sitting in the corner. They were wearing white face makeup and using hand gestures and pantomime to communicate. When John and Barbara were seated the mimes stopped what they were doing and they all looked over at them. They then hunched over and kept making gestures but it was much less animated. John looked at them and thought how strange that was. It was almost like they were trying to whisper. One of them looked up and gave John a cold stare. He took his finger and slid it across his neck. John quickly looked down into his menu.

The waiter approached the table "Tonight's specials are the Herring Pad Thai, Reindeer curry with coconut milk and lingonberries and lutefisk with mangoes and passion fruit."

John was trying to make heads or tails from the menu. "What is Medisterkaker?"

The waiter stood there thinking "I, I don't know."

"How could you not know what's on your menu?"

"No one has ever ordered that before."

"Couldn't you ask the chef?"

"We're not allowed to talk to the chef. He gets very angry if anyone talks to him."

"Could I talk to him?"

"You really don't want to do that sir."

John thought it was too long of a day to make an argument over this. "Interesting you're able to get reindeer out here." The waiter got a nervous look and started to shift his eyes and then put his head down. John didn't notice any of this, he was still looking at the menu. "Ok, I'll try the reindeer curry."

"Very good, sir. And for the lady?"

Barbara looked up at the waiter "Jeg vil ta juleskinke." The waiter stood there frozen looking at Barbara as if she was from another planet. Barbara smiled "I will take the juleskinke." The waiter still looked confused. "Christmas ham, see juleskinke" as she pointed to the item on the menu.

The waiter scribbled something down on his pad. "Yes ma'am." He quickly grabbed the menus and walked into the kitchen.

John was very impressed. "I didn't know you know how to speak Norwegian?"

"I don't, only a few phrases. I can learn a language very quickly when I want to. It's just something that I can do."

The waiter came back over to the table with a basket. John looked at the bread; it was a twisted loop like three quarters of an infinity symbol. The color was a dark green almost black. "What is this?"

"It's berlinerkranser made with grass jelly."

"How good is it?" John inquired. "Does it taste good?"

"Depends on how much you like the taste of iodine." replied the waiter who then walked away.

John picked up a piece, was just about to try it and then put it back down. "Did you study foreign languages in school?"

"Oh no," Barbara replied, "I didn't have time to waste on that."

"What did you get your degree in?"

"I majored in electrical engineering and minored in statistics. After my bachelors I got my MBA."

"Wow!" John exclaimed. "That's really impressive to study that -- is it me or is this music ear splitting?" Over the ceiling speakers the music had been loud and distorted but now it was full of screaming like someone was being stabbed to death. At this point the waiter came out of the kitchen again holding two bowls.

"Please enjoy the appetizer, our fusion version of torsk med eggsaus."

John looked in the bowl and saw a bunch of white items with black spots and something that looked like walnut shells. "What is in here and secondly, can you please turn down the music?"

"It's codfish, butter, durian, peppercorns and walnuts."

John looked closely at the bowl and got an aroma that made his eyes tear. "Can something be done about the music?"

"I don't think so; it's the chef's favorite band. I don't think he will turn it down, he never does."

John was feeling a migraine coming. "What is it? Is this the soundtrack to *The Exorcist*?"

"The band is Gorgoroth. I think it's off the Under the Sign of Hell album. Sounds like Krig."

"You understand that?"

"No, it's just when you hear the same album for six weeks straight you begin to recognize it." The waiter walked away from the table again.

John called to the waiter, "Can I get some more water?" The waiter turned to look back at John and nodded.

John looked at the appetizer and found it less than appetizing. He turned his attention towards Barbara again. "So what made you study engineering then business?" Barbara just looked at John with a sly grin, her head slightly tilted. "Ok, I got it. Funny how you don't say much but somehow you say so much by not saying anything, but you didn't say it I'm babbling, I don't think that made any sense."

Barbara smiled. "I have noticed that nothing I never said ever did me any harm."

John was amazed. "That's so profound. I should try that sometime."

"It was Calvin Coolidge who said that. Another of his quotes that is my favorite is you can't know too much, but you can say too much."

The waiter came back with another glass of water and put it on the crowded table. John looked at him with a puzzled look. "Aren't you going to fill my empty glass, why bring me another one."

"You can always pour it into your other glass if you want." The waiter thought for a second, "It is a free country." The waiter quickly turned and left again.

"So getting an engineering degree allows you to understand what the business does and the MBA allows you to run it one day." John got concerned for a moment. "Does this mean you know how the technicians do their job?" She nodded. "So when I make a mistake and try and play it off..." John trailed off and saw that Barbara was giggling. His mind started to drift on how adorable she is, how smart, great sense of humor...

"Please enjoy the house specialty soup" the waiter slammed down a large bowl on the table and put out four smaller serving bowls. John realized that the waiter had not taken away any plates but kept bringing things out. The table by now was already full.

"Dare I ask what is in the soup?" John sarcastically asked.

"Banana, basil and moose antler." The waiter turned to walk away.

"Excuse me, excuse me", John was trying to get the waiter's attention. The waiter turned back and looked at John. "Are you going to remove any of the plates we are finished with?"

"That's not my job, I only serve. I'll get someone out here to do that."

John looked at Barbara. "Tell me about you."

Barbara looked at John with a direct focus, staring into his eyes deeply. John realized that this wasn't how she normally looked at him, she looked different. As if she was opening a locked door and was going to allow him to come inside. "I started working at the company when I was fourteen. It was right after my mother died in a car accident. I would come in after school and would answer phones and learn how to manage the office. It was what my mother did since my dad started the company just before I was born. Help was needed to run the office and handle the phones."

"Who would answer phones before you arrived after school?"

"Fred would answer the phones before I got in."

"I cannot imagine that, must have been a nightmare."

Barbara chuckled "Yes, he was not good at

answering phones. But as I learned the job I decided I want to be able to carry on in my father's footsteps."

At this point the waiter brought out their dinners. There was no room on the table, the waiter piled plates on top of one another and balanced their dinners on top of other plates. John wanted to mention that he suspects that her father may not be the most honest of businessmen, about how he is buying equipment with eels inside of them, why he's never in the office. But he thought that this would ruin this moment. He didn't want to upset her. This was the most she had said to him in the past seven years that he has been working with her.

"I know what it's like to lose a mother; mine died when I was nineteen from a heart attack. My father went the same way months later." Barbara reached across the table and grabbed his hand. "Since I was in college I became more focused and pushed myself to get a degree and to make a living in technology. Everyone wanted me to become a computer programmer but I hated it, I wanted to work hands on. It was as if no one was listening to me." John got a devilish smile on his face. "I mean, I didn't appreciate people giving me the Spanish Inquisition.

Barbara suddenly got a huge smile on her face. "Nobody expects the Spanish Inquisition! Our chief weapon is surprise, surprise and fear, fear and surprise, our two weapons are fear and surprise and ruthless efficiency. Our three weapons are fear, surprise and ruthless efficiency and an almost fanatical devotion to the Pope. Our four, no, amongst our weapons, amongst our weaponry, are such elements as fear, surprise, I'll come in again."

John was blown away. He had been using that joke for years hoping that someone would pick up on it. Once a woman he was dating started to argue with him for being blasphemous. That relationship didn't last long. But this was different; he now knew that he was in love with her. The waiter brought out two flaming bowls and attempted to put them down on the table full of plates, bowls and glasses that were never bussed. The flames burned intensely and by the time the bowls were set down on something that wouldn't topple them, everything was burned to a crisp. During this process the gloves the waiter was using caught on fire. He threw them office onto the ground and started to stomp on them to put out the flames.

John looked at Barbara, "Think it's time to go to the movie." She nodded in agreement. They arrived at the building a few minutes later; Albert was outside greeting everyone who arrived. "I'm so glad the two of you made it." he said to John and Barbara. "Please go inside and get a good seat and help yourself to some toasted quinoa."

Inside were about two dozen chairs set in front of a large sixty inch monitor. There were five people already seated in various seats, John didn't recognize anyone. No one looked at him or Barbara; they found two seats in a middle row and sat down. A few more people came in and sat down silently.

Albert walked up to the front. He was now wearing a long purple cape. "My name is Albert McKinney and I want to welcome you all to the Philolaus Society monthly Christmas party and the debut of my new film *The Agony of the Tooth.* I am honored for all of you to be here today. This project has been a dream of mine for many years and the fact that I get to show it to you tonight..." he paused, voice cracking in deep emotion as if he was ready to cry, "is something..." attempting to hold back the tears, "that makes me very proud." He took a deep breath, wiped his eyes. "My goal was to make a Hans Richter style of movie," his voice was back under control "and I want to dedicate it to my favorite filmmaker Kenneth Anger. So Gustav, please turn down the lights, I'm going to hit play on the DVD. Please enjoy and we will have a discussion when the movie is over."

The film started with a man walking down a street with a handful of papers. He walks into a store with the sign Scandinavian Printing. He walks up to the counter and a man on the other side turns to him. He asks if he can be of service but at the bottom of the screen is an algebraic equation. The customer responded and had a complaint which gave a much more complex math equation subtitle. Each item spoken had a combination of square roots, derivatives; John thought he saw a quadratic equation tossed in at one point. The customer was angry that he gave them a job to copy and they changed it to Swedish and now he can't read it.

Besides being thoroughly confused, John started to feel tired. He was scared that he would doze off. Seeing how he didn't get much sleep last night and had a stressful day with a lot of emotional ups and downs, he was ready to collapse. Barbara, who was sitting to his right, reached over and took his hand. She then rested her head on his shoulder. John thought that this should help keep him awake. The next thing he noticed was that the scene was completely different, someone was standing in a supermarket aisle holding up plastic salad dressing bottles and then releasing them to fall and bounce on the ground. He realized that he might have dozed off. When he looked at the screen again a man was standing on top of a car waving a golf club over his head screaming on the top of his lungs and a caption came across the screen End of Part I. No doubt about it now he thought, I definitely fell asleep. He hoped that no one noticed and then he realized that Barbara would have obviously have noticed. But she didn't wake him. If there weren't enough reasons for him to fall in love with her today, this solidified it.

The lights came on and John wiped his face, feeling numb from taking a nap which he thought lasted a few minutes but turned out to be a few hours. He still felt groggy and wanted to make sure he stayed awake with the lights on. He looked at Barbara who looked back at him, smiled and then squeezed his hand. Albert stood up in front of the audience. "So, what do you think?"

"I found it to be compelling" a man sitting a few rows behind John spoke. "It felt like a loose interpretation of *Death of a Salesman*, very loose."

"Was the scene with the yak necessary?" a woman up front commented.

"Oh, of course." Albert replied. "It is the most important scene in the film. It is the underlying purpose of the film. Without out the scene with the yak the entire film loses its significance."

"But what does it mean?" the woman responded.

"The yak represents prosperity." another man in the audience commented.

Albert thought for a second, "No, that's not the message I was going for. Although I understand why you could see it that way. But that wasn't my goal."

Barbara spoke up. "The yak is a symbol of life. It represents the struggle of man against machine, his dependence on technology, his fear of death. The yak is the unifying theme that brings everything together." John looked at Barbara awestruck and thought to himself that maybe he shouldn't have slept throughout this film.

"Yes!" Albert screamed. "Yes, that is exactly the point I was trying to make. She gets it." Albert ran towards Barbara and grabbed her head with both hands. "You are my soul mate. You know me better than anyone else." He then kissed Barbara on her forehead. "You are a genius."

As he walked away John looked at Barbara with a jealous look. She gently shook her head and whispered, "I'll explain later." John was concerned, but he was too tired to get up and walk out. Albert continued to speak but John wasn't listening. He started to doubt himself and wondered if he was a fool for falling for Barbara.

A few minutes later Albert thanked everyone, encouraged everyone to take a few bags of toasted quinoa home with them and while walking to the DVD player tripped on his cape. As they walked out Barbara slipped her arm around John's arm and put her head against his arm.

John opened the car door for Barbara and she got in. Walking around the back of the car he saw through the rear window Barbara leaning over to open the driver side lock. John remembered the movie *A Bronx Tale* and thought for a second maybe she is the one?

As soon as John closed the door Barbara spoke. "I know what you're thinking and it's not the case."

"I'm not thinking about anything."

"I saw the look on your face. You have nothing to be jealous of. Albert is not what you think."

"You mean he's on the other team?"

"No, he's not gay. He and I have a close relationship from working together. He has told me that he loves me like an older sister. So there's nothing there."

John started driving and didn't say anything for a few minutes. "So are you seeing anyone right now?"

"Nope."

"You might be interested in going on another date?"

"I might." Barbara said with a smile.

A few minutes later John pulled up in front of Barbara's apartment building. He turned to her. "Should I come up?"

"Not tonight, but soon." She then leaned over and kissed John on the lips. "Get home safe. See you on Monday." John watched her walk up the stairs of the apartment building, open the door and walk inside. He waited for the door to shut and sat there for a minute looking up at the building wondering which apartment was hers. John then drove away.

A few blocks from her apartment John heard a police siren and looked in his rear view mirror and saw a motorcycle cop waving for him to pull over. John couldn't think of anything he had done wrong. He was following the speed limit, the car was new so all the tail lights are working, he wasn't driving erratically. The officer swaggered up to the car and tapped on the window. John lowered the window. "Yes, officer, is there something wrong?"

"Sir, what I'm going to need for you to do for me ok right now is to show me your license ok right now and your registration ok right now." John leaned over and took the registration out of the glove box and handed it to the police officer with his driver's license. "Sir, I'm also going to need for you to do for me right now, ok, is to real quick ok right now your insurance, ok right now, ok, sir, ok if you can do that ok right now."

John handed the insurance card to the police officer. "Officer, could you please tell me if I did something wrong?"

The police officer looked at the documents, looked over his shoulder, back at the documents, looked ahead of him into the darkness, back to the documents, down at his feet, looked at John and then back to the documents. "What I'm going to need from you sir, ok right now, I'm going for you ok to get the required temporary license, ok right now. Right now, ok sir, you don't have a license plate, ok right now. You'll need sir to obtain a temporary license and properly display it in your rear window, ok right now."

"Officer I do have a temporary license, it's in the rear window."

The police officer got a confused look on his face, looked around him and then into the car. He shined his flashlight on the rear window. "Sir, ok right now I see that you are in compliance right now ok, with your temporary license. Right now it's not easy to see, ok right now, ok right now, so you may be pulled over again, ok right now. So I'm going to need for you to do for me ok right now is to put your license plate on when it arrives." The police officer leaned out of the car but did not turn off his flashlight which he shined into John's eyes.

"Yes, officer, I will. Can I get back my license?"

The police officer looked confused, looked down at the documents in his hand and then handed them back to John. "Ok, sir, I'm going to need for you to drive safe for me right now ok right now." He tapped on the roof of the car and walked back to his motorcycle.

John turned on his turn signal and slowly pulled away from the curb. He drove another two blocks and saw the police lights in his rear view mirror again. He pulled over the first open space he could find. The same police officer got off his motorcycle. John checked to see if the officer gave him back all of his paperwork, he couldn't think of any other issue. The police officer walked over to the passenger side of the car and tapped on the window. John lowered the window. "Sir, ok right now sir it appears that you are not properly operating your vehicle that you are driving ok right now. You are sitting on the wrong side ok for me right now."

"Officer, you are on the passenger side." The police officer looked around him and started to walk towards the front of the car. He turned sharply to his left but didn't clear the front of the car and walked into the front hood on the side of the car. He turned to his right and then walked around the front of the car and came up to the window and looked at John.

"Sir what I'm going to need for you to do for me right now, I need for you to ok right now show me your driver's license real quick ok right now." John handed him his license, registration and insurance. The police officer looked surprised. "Thank you for being efficient right now ok sir. So you know why I pulled you over ok right now this evening sir right now?"

"I'm not sure, but is it because I don't have a license plate yet and you couldn't see me temporary license?"

The police officer stared at John and then turned his head to the left and stared for what seemed to be a long time. "Ok, yes sir, right now I pulled you over for not having a proper license on your vehicle of operation right now ok."

"That's what you pulled me over for about two minutes ago."

The police officer stood there looking confused. "Sir, ok right now, I'm going to have to ask you to show me right now ok that you right now ok have a temporary license right now."

John pointed over his left shoulder. "It's in the back of the rear window."

The officer looked in, didn't use his flashlight this time. "Ok sir, thank you, ok right now. You may get pulled over again ok until you get your license plate ok right now."

"I know, that's what you told me the last time you pulled me over."

The police officer handed back John his paperwork. "Ok sir, I want to you to drive safe now ok sir."

John watched the police officer walk back to his motorcycle and drive off. He got about another block before he saw the same cop wave for him to pull over. He thought to himself that this is getting ridiculous. He waited for the police officer to come up to his window and handed everything to him before he could say anything. "Don't tell me, officer, but is this about my temporary license not being visible?"

The police officer stood in a daze holding John's information without looking at it, just staring over the top of the car. He then looked down at John. "Sir, no, ok right now I need to see your driver's license. You sir ok right now are driving without a proper license plate on your vehicle ok right now."

John looked closely at the police officer and noticed that there was blood trickling down the side of his face from under his helmet. "Officer are you ok, have you been in an accident?"

The police officer got very tense like standing at attention. He looked at John. "I am not afraid of you filthy mimes. You won't get me a second time." The police officer stared at John with a frightened look on his face and then quickly looked over his shoulder and then back at John. "Sir are you aware it's a felony to ask a police officer a question.

"No sir, it is not." The police officer just stared at John without saying anything. John realized he needed to get away from this guy before he pulls out his firearm. "Thank you for the warning officer. My license and insurance?" The police officer handed it back to John slowly in a numb zombie like fashion. He then walked back to his motorcycle.

John waited until he started it up and made a U-turn and went in the opposite direction. He decided to turn off the major street and take side streets to get back to his apartment building. About a block from his apartment he saw police lights in his rear view mirror from the same motorcycle cop. He pulled over and put his head down on the steering wheel.

Chapter Five

John was standing in his elementary school playground. There were buckets of water and paper bags, the small lunch size, with the tops rolled down filled with water as well. He was supposed to dump the water in a bin where a sign was above it saying you must put water here. John decided to kick over the bags and buckets of water. He picked up one of the paper bags and tossed it in the lap of the guy who played Luis on Sesame Street who was sitting on a bench. John laughed and started to run away. He thought that this must happen to him often and must be prepared for this. He looked back at him and saw that he wasn't moving but had a maniacal grin on his face.

John ran across the street and then looked over his shoulder. He noticed that Luis was reaching into a bag of eggs and threw one at John. He was a good forty to fifty feet away from John and it went flying a good ten feet over John's head going very fast. John then ran across a four lane road with a large island in the middle. To his left was swamp land all fenced up. He turned to his right to see another egg go flying way over his head. Luis then handed an egg to the woman who played Maria on Sesame Street who threw an egg that fell short of John. Luis then handed one to one of the puppets whose throw only made it half way across the street. He then threw an egg that looked like it bounced but then splattered and hit the back of John's right leg. John looked at his leg and saw nothing on it but it hurt.

"You still can't hit me," John yelled at them. He noticed that they were now at the island in the middle of the street and John started to get tired. He was pulling himself along on the fence next to the swamp and thought that this is strange. He could easily run home without getting tired. He turned back and saw that they were very close to him and decided on a new strategy. Luis was now a kid and John started to catch the eggs. The first one went by John, the second one he caught and threw back hitting Luis causing him to fall. The next one John threw hit him too and he was then lying in the middle of the street. John turned the corner and ran into his house and went half way up the stairs and saw that someone was at the door. His mother walked out of the kitchen and said she would get the door.

John opened his eyes and saw that it was five minutes to six. He tried to think what would bring about a dream of that magnitude but decided to try and forgot about it. He also realized that he won't be able to get back to sleep. And if he did get back to sleep, what if the dream continued or worse the cast of *Maude* chased him with guavas. Might as well get up and check my email he thought.

John saw he got an email from Joseph last night. He said he tried calling John but since he didn't answer sent him an email. He wanted to know if John wanted to come over to his parents for dinner on Saturday, his mom's insistent so John was not to have no as an answer. Said to meet him at Captain Tony's bar for a beer before dinner at six thirty and he wanted him to look over a poem that he had been editing for next Friday. John looked at the poem and tried to make sense of it.

> Fred the goat is dead
> He went out drinking last
> And then he died
> And now he's dead
> And outside my window
> I hear them chanting

Kill the tree people
And I went into this really big store
It was a supermarket
And had everything from caviar
To premade heroes
To doughnuts and different types of
bread
Yet there was no peanut butter
It's not like I really care
I personally hate peanut butter
But you would think a store half a mile
long and wide
Would have peanut butter
But they don't
I saw someone come in
With a jar of peanut butter
They smuggled it in
And had it rung up at the register

John read it a few times and it still didn't click with him. He thought that maybe everyone else gets it but not him. Just like last night when he didn't understand the movie. But then again he did sleep through three hours and twenty two minutes of it. Either way he was looking forward to dinner with Joseph's parents because his mom is a very good cook. It would also be good to talk to Joseph about Barbara as well.

John decided to watch some television to relax. He turned on the classic movie channel and they were showing one of his favorite comedies of the 1930's, *Ruggles of Red Gap*. He sank into the couch and started to feel drowsy. John thought that he should get up and make some coffee.

John looked around him and saw that he was on a game show set. A man in a bright green suit walked out, grabbed a microphone and put his arm around John's shoulder. "All right everyone; let's get ready to play our favorite game, What's My Shoe Size? I'm Biff Winkington, your host. Tonight our contestant is John Warsley. John is an engineer technician who is playing for five thousand dollars. Are you ready, John?"

John looked shocked and surprised. He tried to speak but no words come out. Biff laughed. "Let's meet our judges. Our first judge is a paint taster from Santa Fe New Mexico who kills small animals in his spare time. Say hello to Bob Planford."

"Hi Biff, great to be here." Bob walked to a table and took the first seat.

"Our second judge is a part time nurse and welder from Omaha, Nebraska who writes threatening letters to kindergarten teachers. Say hello to Becky Tork."

"Thanks for having me on the show, Biff." Becky walked over to the table and sat in the middle chair to the left of Bob.

"And our third judge is an author from Youngstown, Ohio; let's give a warm welcome to Frank Knarf."

"Thanks Biff, but I should correct you I'm not an author, I write in books."

"Isn't that the same thing?" Biff asked.

"No, I write in books already written." Frank responded.

"That's great Frank."

"I've been thrown out of most of the libraries in Youngstown."

"Save it for the final round Frank. Ok John, let's throw our first question at you. What is the square root of an egg if Korean veterans have too much yarn and the carrot lady is looking for her blue purple cat?"

John looked up at the studio lights, over at the cameras and then at Biff. "Orange seven and the flame thrower lighter."

Biff looked at his index card. "That's correct! Torgo,

tell John what he has won."

A voice came from an overhead speaker "He's won the thirty seven volume of *The History of Boiled Vegetables* as narrated by Lorne Greene on VHS. And a box of dead lizards."

Biff patted John on the back. "Great job, John, now take off your shoes and don't forget about the yak."

John's eyes popped open and he realized he was still in his living room. He decided that he should get up now and make some coffee so he wouldn't fall back asleep again.

...

John arrived at the bar and found Joseph inside sitting at a table. He noticed that the bar was small and there were a number of people who were wearing jackets with a large Km in a circle with a red slash through it. John sat at the other side of the table from Joseph who was busy writing in a notebook.

"Didn't see you come in there, buddy." Joseph looked up and noticed John sitting across from him. "Let me get you a drink. Waitress?" He waved to a waitress on the other side of the bar.

A young woman with blond hair and a nice smile came over. "What would you like?"

John thought for a second. "I'll take a bourbon Manhattan."

Joseph made a concerned face. "You can't order that."

"Why, isn't this a bar? Don't they have a liquor license?" John asked somewhat confused at the situation.

The waitress responded. "I'm sorry sir; we don't serve any alcohol that comes in a metric container."

John thought this was too funny, but realized that

she was serious. "Then what do you have?"

"We have beer, mead and a homemade version of soapberry wine that tastes a bit like shoe polish."

John looked at the waitress "I'll take a beer please."

"Good choice sir. Another one for you sir?"

"No, no thank you." Joseph replied. He looked back at John. "So where were you on a Friday night?"

"I was on a date."

"Anyone I know?"

"Don't think so. I work with her."

"You do anything fun?"

"Went to dinner and then saw a film that someone at work made."

"Was the movie good?"

"No, no it wasn't. To be honest I fell asleep at the beginning of the film and woke up at the end. But that's not important. I think I have some big news."

The waitress returned with John's beer and put a bowl of almonds on the table.

"So do I." Joseph thought for a second. "Why don't you go first?"

John was about to speak then paused. "I think she may be the one."

"Just after one date?" Joseph gave John a look that could be read as are you serious.

"Don't give me that look. Yes, I think I'm serious about her."

"You met her at work. How long have you been working with her?"

"As long as I've been there, seven years now."

"And after all that time you now think you're falling in love with her?"

"I've wanted to ask her out for a while but never had the courage until yesterday. But something happened at dinner that blew my mind. You know my Spanish Inquisition joke?"

"Yes, I've heard it."

"You know how I mention everyone wanted me to become a computer programmer but I didn't want to and I would get the Spanish Inquisition."

"It was funny the first fifty times I heard it."

"I made the joke, as I normally do when I talk about my studies." John paused and gripped his beer tightly. "She smiled and then she recited Cardinal Ximenes's opening speech."

Joseph had a look of shock on his face, as if he had seen a ghost. "Seriously?" John nodded. "Wow. That's, that is amazing. Dude, you need to marry her."

"I think it's a little bit soon to think about marriage."

"No, you need to marry a chick like that. That is a perfect woman. You don't marry her, I'm going to marry her."

"You've never met her. You don't know what she looks like."

"I don't care. I bet she knows the entire *Holy Grail* word for word as well."

"I want you to meet her. I'm going to ask her to join me at your event next Friday." John took a sip from his beer. He reached into the bowl and saw that the almonds were still in the shell. He looked towards the bar and got the attention of the bartender. "Can I get something to open these with, a nutcracker please?"

"We don't have any," the bartender responded.

"Then what should I use?" John was a bit annoyed.

The bartender shrugged and turned away. John took his beer glass and attempted to smash the almond open. It didn't work. The bartender turned and shouted at John. "Hey, don't damage my glass."

"Sorry." John responded as he put his glass back down as he looked back at Joseph. "So what's you're big news?"

"Well not as big as yours, but next week I've been

asked to give the opening poem at Saturday's --"

Joseph stopped as everyone looked at the front door where a mime walked in. He sat down at the bar and pantomimed pulling a cork from a bottle with his teeth, pouring it into an imaginary glass and then taking the glass and drinking it, throwing his head back.

Joseph whispered to John, "We better leave, this may get ugly." The men wearing the jackets with the Km with a red slash in it walked past their table and surrounded the mime.

John whispered back to Joseph "Who are those guys?"

"That's the local Anti-Metric System League." Joseph looked concerned. "You don't want to mess with those guys. Someone I know as a joke went up to them and told them the temperature in Celsius and one of them punched him in the face."

The bartender walked up to the mime and leaned in his face. "You better leave. We don't serve your kind here."

The mime smiled and then looked around him. He then took his fist and pretended to wipe tears from his eyes. He stood up and waved goodbye to everyone. As he opened the door he pretended that the wind blew him back, but he got his footing and walked out.

One of the men in the crowd spoke up. "We ought to go after him and beat him up." A few in the crowd opined agreement. One with a mustache who appeared to be the leader spoke, "No, let him go. He won't be coming back here again."

Joseph looked at his watch. "We better go, don't want to be late for dinner." He walked up to the bar and paid the bill, making sure the bartender saw that he left a generous tip. The bartender nodded to him, Joseph nodded back.

As they walked out John looked at Joseph. "What

was that all about?"

Joseph sighed. "I'll tell you later. Don't mention this to my parents; they have a tendency to worry."

...

John awoke Sunday morning refreshed. He thought being with Joseph's family and eating a good meal can do a lot for your overall psyche. After he got dressed he decided to out and get a newspaper.

Walking down the street John thought it would be good to get a cup of coffee, read the paper, do the crossword and just relax. A car pulled up to the curb and lowered the passenger side window. William leaned over and called to John.

John walked up to William's car and leaned down to the window. "What are you doing around here today?"

"I was on my way to my uncle's factory. I could use your help."

"I don't want to move anything."

"It's not moving anything. I just need someone to watch my car when I'm inside. It's not a good neighborhood and I don't want any junkies ripping off my stereo."

"I don't know, I was going to get a cup of coffee and read the paper."

"I'll buy you a cup of coffee."

"Well..." John was hesitating.

"Come on, it's not like I'm keeping you from finding the cure for cancer. Help me out."

John realized he didn't have much of a defense so he nodded his head and got into the car.

"Where are we going? Where is this place?"

"It's south of here, not in a good neighborhood. I don't want to be there alone. Thanks buddy, I appreciate it."

They drove for a few minutes. John was wondering why he was in the car with William. "So why do we have to go to your uncle's factory on a Sunday morning?"

"He called me and said I have to get something for him from his office."

"What would he need that he couldn't get himself?"

"I don't know. He called me and asked me to do him a favor. I don't question, he's my uncle. He said it would be on his desk and I would know what it is. Ok?"

"It's ok." John backed off; he didn't want to get into a fight with William, especially when he's this far from home. "We'll help out your uncle."

"Thanks buddy, I owe you one." William was quiet for about a minute. "So how bad was Albert's movie?"

"It was a train wreck. I slept through the entire thing."

"Saw that you took Barbara to the movie. How was that?"

"It was great. We had a good time. Um, you know, I really don't want to talk about that."

"I'm just saying she's really nice and you two --" William turned his head to see that John was staring at him with a bit of a scornful look on his face. "It's cool; it's none of my business."

Around ten minutes later they pulled up on a gravel road to an old factory that looked abandoned. "This is your uncle's factory?" John questioned.

"Yeah, why?"

"It looks like it hasn't been used since World War II. What was it? A munitions factory that had a workplace accident?"

"You think this is bad, you should see his house." William pulled a set of keys from his pocket and tried to open the door. None of them fit. "Looks like he gave me the wrong keys."

"I thought he called you?"

William looked nervous. "He did. I got these from him the other day. You know I think these are for the back entrance. I'm going to go in the back. I need for you to keep a lookout to make sure no one comes near the car."

"And if they do?"

"No one will. But if they do, just call me. I'll hear you. You'll be fine."

John looked around him and saw no other buildings or houses. There was an open area full of bricks and garbage, as if a building was demolished. He looked closer and it appeared to have been burned to the ground. He looked around and saw that almost everything had been burned, trees, buildings, even an attempt to burn the bricks. William came running back to the car holding a few reams of printer paper. He handed them to John "Can you take these?"

"This is what your uncle wanted? He couldn't go to the mall and buy some paper there?"

"I don't know. The family is getting worried about him; they think he's losing his mind. Come on let's get out of here, I'll get you a cup of coffee."

"Do you smell something burning?"

"No. A lot of houses out here have wood burning stoves, that's what you're smelling."

"But there aren't any houses out here."

"You know the smell lingers. Let's go before I leave you here." John got into the car and William raced off. John didn't look behind him but smoke started to billow out of the factory and then burst into flames. By this time William was far enough away that John would never notice.

As they were driving back into town William's phone rang. He looked at it with a panicked look and looked over at John who didn't notice. By the third ring John spoke up. "Aren't you going to answer it?"

"Hello?" William answered tepidly. "Oh hello uncle, how are you?" John couldn't make out what William's uncle was saying but it sounding like someone angrily shouting into the phone. "Yes uncle, I got your stuff from the factory office. The factory office. The factory? Right, I got your stuff from the factory. No, no I'm with my friend John. No uncle, he's cool, he helped me out." William put the phone to the side and turned to John. "Uncle says hi." He put the phone back to his ear. "Yes uncle. I know. But, but, I see, I got you. Ok, I'll head over now." He hung up the phone. "Sorry I'll have to offer you a rain check on the coffee, I have to go over to my uncle's house now."

"Is everything ok?"

"Oh yeah, it's all good. Are you near to where we are?"

"I'm about three blocks from here, you can let me out." John got out and realized that he was still holding the reams of paper. "Oh wait your uncle's paper."

"You can have them if you want."

"What am I going to do with your uncle's paper? Isn't this what we went there for?"

"Right, right, what am I thinking? I'll take those." William proceeded to throw the reams of paper into the back seat. "See you tomorrow" and then he sped off.

John thought that was pretty strange. He walked a few blocks until he saw a coffee shop. He went to open the door and it was locked. He saw someone was inside so he knocked on the glass window. Someone walked up to the window and shouted "What?"

"Are you open?"

"No, we're closed."

"But your sign says you're open twenty four hours."

"Yeah, but not in a row." He then walked away from the window. John decided to cut his losses and just go back to his apartment.

...

John arrived to work on Monday in a good mood, something that felt like an alien concept to him. He was glad to see Barbara sitting at her desk when he walked in. "Good morning," he said to her. Barbara smiled and reached out and squeezed his hand. "What are you doing this Friday?"

"I'm giving a speech at the United Nations," she smiled and gave John a wink.

It caught him off guard for a second. "Well, cancel that, you'll be with me at the Café Wombat. My best friend will be the main poet that night. I want you to meet him. And I'd to like to go out again too, of course."

Barbara smiled. "I guess I'll have to cancel that then."

"I'll pick you up at six?" John asked.

"No, I'll pick you up at six. Better be ready." Barbara gave John a wink.

Albert walked in and saw John and Barbara. "Thank you two again for being at my film premiere. I felt good about it. You know I can give you a copy of the DVD if you like if you want to watch it again?"

John thought for a moment. "Why don't I wait for the second half of the film and I can watch it just before to get me back up to speed."

"It's a trilogy" Albert proudly proclaimed, "and the first part was the shortest one. I think the next one may be eight hours. I should be getting started next month." He then walked over to his desk just in time to avoid seeing the pained look on John's face as if he bit into a lemon. John shook his head, smiled at Barbara and walked into the technicians' area.

He walked past William who was attentively working on his computer. He was working with purpose as if he was in a hurry. "How is your uncle doing?"

"What uncle?" William was confused for a second. "Oh right, my uncle. Um, he's doing, um, fine."

"What happened to your hand?" John noticed a large bandage wrapped around William's right hand. It looked like someone had smashed it with a brick.

"This, oh nothing, it's fine. Say you better be on the lookout, I think Tim wants to have a staff meeting." William went back to frantically typing to finish up what he was doing so he could leave.

"You know that reminds me of a strange dream I had last night. You and I were at some customer site and you kept getting into fights with the customer. I was in another room when I heard a gunshot. I came in and you were bleeding from the right side of your head, the bullet grazed you." John thought for a second. "I don't know what it means, but you better be careful out there today.

"You were supposed to dream that two weeks ago." John turned around and saw Fred who just said that and was now staring at him. He was reaching into the coffee creamer container with his hands and then eating it. "Well there goes having any coffee, unless we have milk?"

"Tell me about it, I wish." William offering up his agreement.

"You shouldn't drink milk; it's not good for you." Tim commented as he snuck into the room without anyone seeing him.

William dropped his head and sighed. "How can milk not be good for you? It's the most natural of all

58

substances out there."

Tim fired back "Well, no other animal drinks milk from another animal."

William responded "No other animal has built the space shuttle either."

Tim ignored William. "I got some important items to go over with you guys this morning. First is about remote work orders. You need to get a signature on the work order."

Since John wasn't able to have a cup of coffee yet, he decided to make Tim's life miserable. "Isn't the point of a remote ticket that we are working remotely and not at the customer site?"

Tim looked confused. "Well, yes technically."

John looked at Tim with an incredulous look. "There's nothing technical about it, remote means you're not at the customer site. You are someplace else talking to the customer on the phone."

Tim struggled for an answer. He meekly replied "Yeah, but still."

John continued in his attack. "So if I am fixing the problem with the customer over the phone, how can I get their signature on a work order?"

"You'll have to go to their location and get them to sign the form."

"Doesn't that defeat the purpose of it being a remote ticket?"

"In what way?" Tim still had a look of confusion on his face.

John sighed. "Look, if we are charging the customer less for not going to their site to fix the problem, why would we have to drive out to their location, spend money on time and gas just to get them to sign a form about a repair that they are already aware is fixed?"

"Well I can't change it." Tim was very defensive. "It's a company policy, that is how it is written. It can't change."

"But Tim," William commented, "you wrote the policies. If there is anyone who can change a policy it would be you."

"We'll agree to disagree on this one. Next item on the agenda is dealing with broken equipment. You cannot say that the equipment is broken anymore. You can let them know it's not functioning properly. You can point out that when it's plugged in it's not working the way it should. But you can't say it's broken."

"Is this another one of your policies?" John asked.

"No. No, it is not." Tim was very defensive, still feeling the sting from his last item being shot down. "This is from Jenkins himself."

William laughed. "How would you know? He's never here." As if on cue, Henry Jenkins walked past the doorway of the technicians' area. William laughed again. "Well, what do you know? Speak of the devil." Tim turned and ran out of the office to find Henry.

Henry Jenkins was walking out of his office with fishing poles under his arm. He stopped when he saw Tim. "What?" he asked in a hurried and annoyed tone. Tim froze, he opened his mouth to speak but nothing came out. "I don't have all day Tom, spit it out."

"It's Tim sir. My name is Tim."

Henry Jenkins was the owner of the company. He started the company thirty years ago by himself and as a skilled engineer built it up to what it is today. Over time he started to delegate responsibilities to others. At some point he hired Tim, a decision he quickly regretted. He avoided his phone calls and emails. He would try to come into the office when he knew Tim wasn't there.

"Mr. Jenkins," Tim finally getting his thoughts

together enough to squeak something out, "we are having a problem with the equipment."

"Forget that," Henry grumbled back "I need for you to make space in the warehouse for the new AE35 units arriving."

"But we've been finding eels in the equipment, Mr. Jenkins. Eels."

"Hmm, eels you say. That makes sense." Henry then walked past Tim as if he wasn't there.

"But what do we do about the eels?"

Henry turned back and thought for a second. "Might as well leave them with the customer."

"Well, well that's, that's what was done. But I think--"

"That's you're problem Tim, don't think. You made a good decision." Henry turned to walk out the door. He walked by Barbara and put his hand on her cheek. "How you doing, kid?" Barbara didn't say anything but just looked up at her father and smiled.

Tim attempted to keep the conversation going. "But Mr. Jenkins--"

"Look Tom, I have to attend to an important meeting today. If you ever become a manager you would understand."

"But I am a manager."

"And in sales. Management and sales, you would understand that..." Henry stopped mid sentence and turned and walked out of the office, quickly jumped into his car and drove off.

John was watching this from the doorway of the technicians' area. He turned back to tell William what had just happened, how Jenkins took Tim down by a peg but William was gone. During the exchange William used the chaos to sneak out of the building. John then thought that he missed his opportunity. He walked back to his desk to try and pack up before Tim came back into the room.

"So John, before you leave," Tim had walked in while John was trying to leave without Tim seeing him, "I want to go over the broken, I mean, not functioning properly equipment policy."

"No problem Tim, I'll just say the equipment is misguided. That way it won't hurt its feelings."

Tim wasn't sure if John was being serious or sarcastic. "I'm not sure what you mean by that?"

"Don't worry; just like your eel decision, you'll come out on top." John had finished packing up and walked past Tim and left the office.

"Ok, good meeting everyone. Meeting is adjourned." Tim looked around and noticed that he and Fred were the only ones in the office. Fred was staring at the floor not moving, Tim wasn't sure if he was breathing. He put his head down in frustration and walked out of the technicians' area.

...

John was led into the customer's equipment room. He had to go down two levels below the basement. When inside the room John noticed the walls were covered with mold. The humidity felt like it was one hundred percent. Over the equipment rack the ceiling tiles were stained from water damage.

"Been having water damage lately?" John asked.

The customer calmly replied, "No, what are you talking about?"

John was a bit surprised and somewhat amused. "The water dripping from the ceiling? The mold on the wall? The water stains on the floor?"

"I have no idea what you are talking about. What water damage? I don't see any water damage."

"Are you kidding me? It's like a sauna in here."

"I don't think so. I feel kind of cold."

John looked at the customer and thought either this guy has no sense of humor or he has the best sense of humor in the world. "Fine, let me look at the equipment." John walked over to the rack. The device looked like it was almost rusted out. "I don't think it's in proper working condition."

"You mean it's broken?"

John paused and thought about Tim's moronic ramblings that morning. "No sir, what I'm saying is that it's not in proper working condition."

"What does that mean? You're saying it's broken."

"I'm not saying that."

"Then what are you saying?"

"I'm saying that, it's not in--"

"Yeah, yeah I know. It's not in proper working condition. That means it's broken."

"When I plug in the equipment it doesn't start. It's not doing what it is supposed to be doing. It's not in a proper working condition."

"Broken?"

John sighed. He grabbed a screwdriver and opened the equipment. As soon as John opened the device about a half a gallon of water poured out and three large eels fell out onto the floor. "Looks like you got eels."

"No, I don't."

John looked at the eels wriggling on the floor and wondered why he came to work today.

Chapter Six

John drove home from work Friday afternoon thinking this was the longest week of his life. He wanted to get home to change. He felt awkward about not getting a bit dressed up last week. He had been looking forward to this date all week long. He wanted to talk to Barbara but didn't want to appear desperate or anxious, so he only talked to her a few times during the week.

As John was driving he noticed something strange. About two blocks ahead he saw a group of mimes scatter and run in different directions. He tried to figure out what they were doing. As he drove past a speed limit sign that was 30 miles per hour that they spray painted 48.28 kilometers per hour over the sign.

John also realized that the more he would think about his relationships the more times it would fall apart. He thought very little about the date but one thing kept nagging at him. Why did Barbara insist on picking him up. All directions lead to one conclusion, she wanted to bring him back to her apartment. He remembered her saying not tonight but soon. That kept repeating in his head. All of a sudden he slammed on the brakes. A cat was running across the street that was on fire.

John was waiting outside his apartment for what felt like hours. He looked at his watch and it was five to six. He had been standing here for fifteen minutes. At exactly six Barbara pulled up to the curb. She rolled down the passenger side window. "Wanna ride, big boy"? and then started to giggle. John thought her giggle was the cutest thing he'd ever seen. He got into the car and they drove over to Cafe Wombat.

When they arrived there was a line of a few hundred people waiting to get in. There was no parking for blocks. They finally found a spot a few blocks away and walked back to the cafe. When they arrived at the front door Joseph was outside waiting for them and he waved to them as they walked towards him.

"Great to see you two. I got VIP passes so you don't have to wait on line. There's a table reserved inside."

"Joseph, I want you to meet Barbara."

Barbara put out her hand, Joseph shook it. "It's an honor to meet you. I've heard very nice things about you." Barbara gave Joseph big smile and nodded. Joseph grinned and looked Barbara square in the eyes. "What is the air speed velocity of an unladen swallow?"

Barbara smiled slyly. "What do you mean? An African or European swallow?"

Joseph gave Barbara a big hug. "I love this woman, she is perfect." He then grabbed John's shoulder. "I approve, brother. Now go on inside and I'll see you after the show."

The doorman opened the door and they walked into the club. An usher took them to a table that was just to the left of the stage. "These look like really good seats," John commented. At the table were two other people. Joseph walked up behind John and Barbara.

"I want you to meet Bill. Bill works with me. And this is Candy, she is a big fan of my poetry." They all shook hands and offered basic greetings to one another. Someone came over and whispered something in Joseph's ear. Joseph nodded. "I have to go now, but I will see you after the show. I hope I have a good show. I don't want them to throw the foam tomatoes."

"They throw foam tomatoes?" John asked.

"Oh yeah," Joseph replied. "It's a tradition here to throw foam tomatoes instead of booing."

"Why do the use foam tomatoes?"

"Because the foam rhubarb didn't throw that well."
He then walked off to behind the stage.

John looked around the room and saw there had to
be at least five hundred people in the club. It was
standing room only, packed in like a cattle car. He
looked over at Barbara and noticed how beautiful she
looked. She looked at him and touched his cheek. He
felt like leaning in for a kiss, the moment seemed
right. All of a sudden the stage lights came on and the
crowd started to cheer. The emcee came out on the
stage.

"Ladies and Gentlemen. It's my honor to introduce
our headline poet tonight. This is a man who has
performed here for over ten years, since he was a
struggling college student. Now he's a struggling CAD
engineer. No seriously, this is his first time being the
headline poet. I want you all to give a warm Cafe
Wombat welcome to Joseph Thompson." The crowd
erupted in applause and cheering. Joseph came out
on the stage and took a bow. He put up his right hand
to signal for everyone to calm down and let him start.

"Oh, I hope he starts with a good one." Candy was
all enthusiastic, practically bouncing out of her seat as
if she was a child going to Disneyland.

Joseph grabbed the microphone and looked to the
ground. "I don't want to kill my pet frog--", the
audience roared with applause and loud cheering.
Candy turned to Joseph and Barbara all excited.
"He's starting with a classic!"

Joseph put his right hand up again and waited for
the audience to quiet down and started again.

> I don't want to kill my pet frog
> I think I'll paint him red instead
> And feed him raw liver
> I'd put him in a swamp with a rock on his
> back

66

No, I can't do that, he may die
Maybe if I gave him an oxygen tank
But it's just a frog
What the hell, I'll kill it

Joseph stepped away from the microphone and thunderous applause filled the club. He walked back and grabbed the microphone with both hands extended out in front of him and leaned forward with his head looking down. John thought to himself looks like he's doing his Jim Morrison impersonation and did his best not to break out in hysterical laughter. Joseph stood that way for almost a minute and then lifted his head back up but his eyes were closed.

The mutant coffee beans are after me
And the web footed monster ate my sister
The killer mailman is back in town
With the killer South Dakotan trolls
And agnostic dwarfs
And a elf stole a Oreo cookie from my pet frog
But the acorns are not ripe
So back to the desert the druids must go
Red elks eating my blueberry muffins
And Tylenol flavored gum

There was standing applause at the end of the poem. Candy turned towards John, her eyes starting to tear up. "Isn't he a genius?" John just nodded. He wanted to say something about how he heard these poems in high school and they didn't make any sense back then. But he realized what good it would do to burst this young girl's bubble. Joseph was ready to start another poem.

The Asparagus man ran over my dog
But no, I don't want any lemons
He ate all the melon balls

And the baby food too
And there's only red cabbage left in the
refrigerator
Applesauce on my shoes
And sirens in the air
Giving subliminal messages for Taco
Bell
For wombat burgers
Commercials eating my brain
Until it looks like a rotten orange and
Swiss
Cheese melted in a pot of wax
What? Oh no! The Asparagus man just
kicked
My door in, and is stealing my Opus
doll!
No, leave Opus alone! Leave my
Opus alone!
And in place of my Opus, he
Left a carrot

John looked over at Barbara and wondered what
she was thinking. She looked like she was having a
good time. She seemed to be attentively listening to
the poems, but he couldn't get a read on her, whether
she was just being polite or if she got it. Again John
wondered why he felt confused. To him it all seemed
crazy, like a strange dream that everyone accepted
but he couldn't. Why was he always fighting the
chaos, he thought what would happen if he just
accepted the chaos and he got a cold shiver. John
looked back at the stage and saw Joseph take a big
swig of water. His shirt was covered with perspiration
and sweat was dripping off his forehead like a
fountain. People were whistling and a few started to
hold up lighters. Joseph grabbed the microphone to
start his next poem.

The Giant Frogmen of Nebraska are in
town
And they go down the street
Singing the frogs of Nebulan
And with them comes
Giant mutated kiwi fruits rolling down the
Street and they stapled green grapes to
My forehead. They stuffed my cat full of
Rice A Roni, and made me give my
English Muffins to my stork
The dwarfless midgets
With no eyes, are handing out pineapple
flavored
Oranges. They also have onion rings
made out
Of toothpaste. And now my fleas
Have dogs, and toothpicks with little
legs are
Running after me. The toads have foot
pain
And I am drinking warm Pepsi with cold
broken
Glass. And all is left are pipes full of
slugs
And books on first aid for stick insects.
And when they left, they vomited on my
cat

Joseph was staring at the ceiling then closed his
eyes. His body went limp as if he would fall over, but
before that could happen he stood up straight and
took a bow. He put the microphone back on the stand,
kissed his fingers and turned his hand out to the
audience, like blowing them a kiss. He turned and
walked off the stage. The crowd was chanting encore.
About thirty seconds later Joseph came back up on
stage and everyone started to cheer wildly.

Candy turned back to John again, "I wonder what he will do as an encore?" John shrugged his shoulders. John looked over at Bill who hadn't said anything since they all sat down. He was sitting there with his arms folded looking like he wasn't having a good time. John felt some slight comfort in that he was not the only one here who wasn't having a good time. He was happy for Joseph. He is his best friend and loves him like a brother, but it puzzled him how so many people could enjoy these insane poems. The clapping had started to die down and Joseph stepped up to the microphone.

> There was once thirty-one wonderful flavors
> Now there are only nine
> And seven of them are different types of chocolate
> The other is herring ripple
> And vanilla, fudge, mocha Swiss cheese
> My friend is lucky
> His Baskin-Robbins has thirty flavors
> But mine only has nine
> I think I'll move
> So I can experience more flavors
> Because I hate chocolate
> Oh so much

Joseph waved to the audience. Someone yelled out we love you Joseph as he was walking off the stage. He turned back and took another bow, waved again and walked off the stage a second time. About a minute later he was over at the table. "I think it went over well?"

John was happy for his friend. He knew he wasn't jealous, but he realized he needed to offer encouragement even if he was confused about how popular Joseph was. "Way to go buddy, great show."

Joseph let out a large smile, "Thank you that means so much."

"You have a terrific talent," Barbara commented. "Your words paint a powerful picture of the abstract realm that speaks volumes of truth."

Candy decided to offer her analysis, too. "Yeah, and it makes you feel, like wow."

Joseph smiled at Candy. "Thank you so much. Bill, did you like the show?"

Bill shook his head up and down. "Excelsior my good sir. Veritable erudite balladry. If you shan't disesteem I aim to proceed to the rathskellar."

John looked at Barbara with a confused look. She leaned over and whispered in his ear "He complemented his poetry and will be heading towards the bar." John looked at Barbara and nodded.

Joseph shook Bill's hand. "Thank you for coming, see you on Monday at work." Bill tipped his fedora as a sign of acknowledgment and walked off into the crowd. Joseph turned back to the rest of the table. "I'll try to get a waiter over here, I'm famished."

Candy got up out of her chair. "I'll do that on my way to the rest room. You sit and relax. You must be wiped out after your show."

Joseph sat down. "Thank you, sweetheart." After Candy walked away he turned to Barbara and John. "She's a great kid."

"Does she work with you?" John asked.

"Yes, she is the receptionist over there at work. Been working there about four months now. Apparently she was in college when she saw me perform here years ago and loves my poetry."

"That's not the only thing she loves," Barbara commented.

Joseph looked at her confused. "What do you mean?"

Barbara smiled. "Nothing, just a woman thing."

Joseph laughed. "No argument there. Say, I have big news. Just found out today that I will be speaking at the anti-metric system rally tomorrow. They want me to recite one of my poems."

"What rally are you talking about?" John asked Joseph.

"It's going to be a big rally; everyone has been talking about it." Barbara turned to John, "It's been all over Facebook, I thought you knew about it?"

"Nope, news to me. Whose house is it going to be held in?"

"Very funny," Joseph responded in a condescending voice. "It's going to be at Howard Roark Park in downtown. We had so many RSVP's it had to be moved out of the Galt Arena."

John looked surprised. "The Galt Arena seats ten thousand people. More than ten thousand are coming to the event?"

"We think it's going to be close to fifteen thousand. And I'm giving the opening poem."

"That's wonderful news Joseph." said Barbara. "How did you get chosen?"

"Well as vice president of Poets Against the Metric System I was picked because our president will be heading to Washington, DC, for the big protest next week at the national mall where they expect over two million people to be there."

John was having a hard time grasping this information. "Let me get this straight. Tens of thousands of people will be in downtown tomorrow to protest the metric system?"

"Yes," Joseph nodded. "Don't you hate the metric system?"

John was surprised by the question. "To be honest, I've never thought about it before. I don't hate or

72

support the metric system. It's just something I've never had an opinion on."

"Well, you better keep your mouth shut in here if you don't want trouble," Joseph warned John.

"John, Joseph is right. The metric system is not practical. For example, in cooking you are using cups and tablespoons which were designed for baking while grams were not. And a meter can only be divided by two or five, where a foot can be divided by two, three, four and six. You ever try and measure a third of a meter?"

Joseph looked at Barbara with amazement and awe. "Have I said that this woman is a genius? You my dear lady are a genius." Barbara started to blush.

Candy came back to sit down and a waiter approached the table. "I'd be happy to take your drink orders."

John knew the answer he was going to get, but he decided to try anyway. "I'd like a bourbon Manhattan, please."

"I'm sorry sir, we stand in solidarity with those opposed to title twenty seven of the code of federal regulations which changed standard bottle sizes to metric. We do have beers on tap and a wide variety of house pruno. I would like to tell you our daily specials. Tonight's soup is goat cheese with Brussels sprouts. The toast of the day is sourdough. And the entree is the panda burger with hakari onion rings."

John was caught off guard. "Did you say panda burger?"

"Yes, sir, I did."

"Is that like a charred burger with mozzarella?"

"No, sir, it's panda."

"Is that made from real panda?"

"It's kind of hard to make it from a stuffed panda."

"I didn't think you could serve panda. Isn't that

against the law?"

The waiter got defensive. "What's it to you? Are you with PETA? You sound like someone who supports the metric system."

Joseph quickly interjected. "No, no, he does not support the metric system. He hates it like all of us here." He turned to John. "John, don't cause trouble here, just get the burger and don't make a scene."

John realized he may have overreacted. "Ok, you know what? I've never had panda before, you've convinced me, I'll try it."

The waiter looked at John. "We're all out of the panda burgers."

John shook his head in disbelief. "If you're out of it, why would you mention it as one of the specials?"

The waiter calmly responded to John. "Cause I just don't like you."

John was shocked. "What kind of answer is that? All right, can we at least order some drinks?"

The waiter thought for a moment. "No." He then turned around and walked away.

"Are you going to use a new poem for the rally tomorrow?" Barbara asked Joseph.

"I don't know." Joseph though for a moment. "I don't have any poems directly about the metric system. I'll see if I can come up with something later tonight."

"Maybe you could talk about all the children that are dying every day from the metric system." Everyone looked at Candy who didn't notice their puzzled glances.

John, savoring the moment, couldn't let an opportunity to give his friend a hard time slip away, chimed in. "Yes, Joseph, why don't you talk about all the children that are dying. That would be so dramatic." Candy's eyes lit up, not realizing the true nature of John's comment.

Joseph didn't have the heart to tell Candy that was probably the dumbest thing he had heard in a long time. And he didn't want to ruin his chances with her later that evening either. "Candy, that is such a good idea, but I wouldn't have the time to do the research before tomorrow. I should of had you around weeks ago."

"But Joseph, didn't you tell me that you only found out today that you were giving your poem tomorrow?" John was not going to let him get off that easy.

Joseph shot John a death glare that without words that said I will get you back for this and with interest. "No, I meant it. You could be my inspiration to write."

"You could be his muse, Candy," Barbara said to Candy.

"Is that like the band?" Candy asked Barbara.

Barbara paused for a second. "Yes, exactly."

Joseph decided to turn the tables and go on the attack against John. "Say, Barbara, has John told you about the time back in high school when he got into a fight with a chair and lost?"

Barbara giggled and looked at John who had a pained look on his face now glaring back at Joseph. "Oh yes, by all means, you must tell me that story."

Joseph looked John. "Shall I tell the story or would you like the honor?" John folded his arms. "I guess I will then. When we were in high school our finance class would usually break up into groups to work on projects. One time we were split up into three groups. I was in one, John another and a friend of ours Barry was in the third group. Barry was such a character. They never put us together in any group."

"Do you blame them?" John was no longer folding his arms and was enjoying hearing this embarrassing story told about him for the umpteenth time.

"No, I don't, thinking back on it now. So I was sitting

in my group not paying attention. I was sitting looking at both of the other groups from my vantage point. John was in a circle to my left, Barry in a circle to my right. The chairs were all arranged in a circle with eight or nine people in them. Barry all of a sudden got up out of his chair, grabbed his books, put the chair back neatly into place and started to walk with determination towards John's circle. John couldn't see this; his back was to Barry's group. Barry walked across the room and punched John as hard as he could in his back and then turned and walked back to his group and sat back down again. John on the other hand fell forward and jumped up to go after Barry but ended up tripping over his chair and fell flat on his face."

"I hit my forehead on the top of the chair and it broke a bunch of blood vessels so a few days later my eye became black like someone punched me," John shamefully admitted.

"That was funny, too. But I thought I was going to die laughing. It was the funniest thing I had ever seen. I asked Barry after class why he did that. He told me that he had no reason except that he thought that it would look really funny to someone who was watching it, so he just did it. The guy was a nutcase."

Barbara was laughing, eyes starting to tear up. She then looked at John with a sympathetic look and caressed his cheek. But she couldn't keep her composure and started to laugh again. "What ever happened to Barry?" she asked.

"He joined the military." Joseph commented. "Haven't seen him since high school. Made it a career and is somewhere in Europe the last I heard."

"Remember he was the one who started public theater?" John was laughing looking at Joseph.

"That's right he did."

Barbara had a sly look on her face. "What was public theater?"

"Public theater," Joseph started, "was Barry's way of acting out scenes in public without people knowing what has going on. Remember his what date is it routine?"

"That was a classic." John responded.

Candy looked puzzled. "What was funny about asking someone what date it is?"

John tried to keep from laughing. "Barry was obsessed with the scene in the beginning of *The Terminator* when Kyle Reese asked the police officer what was the date and he told him and then started to demand what year is it. Barry thought that it would be funny to do that and then freak out like they are a time traveler. We would all go to different bus stops and get on one at time and sit apart from each other. Barry would be the last to get on. He would come up to me and ask me "What is the date." He would then start yelling at me to tell him the year. Then he would demand that I tell him who is the king and he would announce that he has eight moons to save the world and he is three moons behind. He would grab me and pull me off the bus with him."

"Then I would jump up and shout that I have the infinity book of magic and can help save the universe and would run off the bus after you two." Joseph wiped a tear from his eye.

"But I still think you losing a fight to a chair is much funnier."

"Funnier than losing a shoe in a mosh pit?" John now turning the tables again.

"I don't know what you are talking about." Joseph stopped smiling getting an embarrassed look on his face.

"Candy, let me tell you a story about Joseph's first

time going to a hardcore punk show. Genius here thought he was going to get beaten to death in the mosh pit. Back in high school Joseph was one hundred and forty five dripping wet."

"It's true. I was much skinnier than I am now, if you could believe that?"

"So Mr. Courage on the hour long drive to the show drank himself to a drunken stupor. But not on beer or vodka, no, but on wine coolers. We get to the show and once the music starts we get separated. A few minutes later I see kamikaze Joe here running head first into skinheads. Guys who are like six foot two and weigh two hundred and seventy pounds are pushing him aside like swatting a fly. He's bouncing around like a pinball. A few minutes after that I ran into Joseph again and he was jumping up and down shouting something. I got closer since I couldn't hear over the music. Joseph while jumping up and down yelled that he lost his show. I looked down and his right shoe was missing. His sock was covered with muddy boot prints. He started to frantically look for his shoe, pushing people aside looking on the ground. I tried to help him but it wasn't in that area. I said let's wait until the end of the show to try and find it. He then went back into the pit with one shoe on."

"Did you find the shoe?" Barbara asked.

John continued. "So we waited until the show was over and everyone left the floor and looked all around for his shoe. We couldn't find it. Someone must have taken it. Our ride was tired and didn't want to wait any longer. But it gets better. When we walked outside it had snowed about eight inches during the show and the car was parked about four blocks away."

Joseph nodded. "I was sobering up at this point and decided to hop on one leg to the car. After about half a block I gave up and just walked to the car in one shoe and my sock."

Everyone was laughing at this point. "Ok truce?"

John put out his hand to shake. "Truce, buddy. Remember we have mutual assured destruction amongst each other." Joseph smiled and shook John's hand.

A man came over and tapped Joseph on the shoulder. Joseph turned to look at him. "Mr. Thompson the manager asked for me to bring you over to the bar for you to sign autographs."

Joseph nodded. "I will be there in just a moment, thank you. John, you going to be here when I get back?"

Barbara interjected "I think we may cut out, I'm not good in big crowds."

Joseph leaned over and gave Barbara a hug. "Well, I'll see you two tomorrow, right?"

Barbara smiled, "Wouldn't miss it for the world. It was great to meet you and you too, Candy." Candy waved to Barbara and John as she walked off with Joseph.

John waited until they walked away and he then turned to Barbara. "If you don't like crowds, why would you want to go to a rally tomorrow?"

She looked at John with a seductive look. "Don't ask so many questions. Why don't you walk me to my car, big boy?"

Barbara drove into her apartment building's underground parking lot. She turned to John. "Why don't you come on up? You didn't eat anything; I can make you some dinner. You must be hungry."

John nodded "Yeah, I am pretty hungry. I'll take you up on that offer."

Chapter Seven

John woke up to the smell of sausage frying. He realized that he wasn't in his bedroom and that he was really hungry from not having anything to eat last night. He stumbled his way out of bed and walked into the kitchen where Barbara was cooking breakfast.

Barbara turned and saw John. "Good morning, Starshine." she then started to giggle.

John looked at Barbara and wondered why she was giggling. He realized that as he grabbed something to wear he got one of Barbara's shirts. He shrugged his shoulders and sat down at the kitchen table. "Stop laughing. Is there any coffee?"

"You just look cute, that's all."

John looked around the apartment. Last night it was rather dark and they ended up in the bedroom almost immediately. It wasn't a large apartment, but was furnished nicely. "Your place is beautiful, much nicer than my apartment."

"I look forward to seeing it soon."

On the wall above the television was a large portrait of a stoic looking man. John didn't recognize who it was. "Who is that a portrait of? Your grandfather?"

Barbara stopped cooking and turned to look at the painting and then at John. "That's Calvin Coolidge, thirtieth president of the United States."

"I thought he looked familiar. I must have seen him in a history book somewhere." John remembered that she quoted Calvin Coolidge on their first date. He thought that she must really like him. The smell of food brought his attention back around to the kitchen. He noticed that she moved with the skill and grace of an artist, like how a painter creates a piece of art. "What are you cooking over there?"

Barbara turned around from the stove. "Some

sausage, home fries and getting the omelets ready. You're not allergic to anything?"

John was amazed. He thought that this is probably the best breakfast he'd ever had. "No, nothing. I can eat a bowl of change."

"We'll worry about lunch later," Barbara quipped.

She set a plate down in front of John that looked beautiful. Everything was placed in an organized and neat pattern on the plate. The aroma was heavenly. She even put a sprig of parsley on top of the omelet. John started to eat like he hadn't had a meal for days. He realized that he might be looking like a savage and forced himself to eat slowly. "This is delicious. When did you learn how to cook?"

"Well, dad doesn't know how to cook," she said between bites, "so after mom died I learned."

John felt awkward for not remembering that Barbara was a teenager when her mother died. But she didn't have a pained look on her face. She was enjoying breakfast. She answered as if he asked her what time it was. He then thought that he could get used to this. He couldn't remember the last time he had a breakfast this hearty. Most mornings he wouldn't eat anything or if he did it was usually a greasy breakfast sandwich or a doughnut. "Well, you are a master. My mom was a good cook but I never learned. Lately most meals I've eaten were either frozen or at some bad restaurant. If it wasn't for Joseph's mom I don't think I'd eat anything good."

Barbara smiled at John and gave him a loving look of appreciation. "Thank you very much."

John thought how nice it is to enjoy a meal. He wasn't sure if it was the food, the company, the calm relaxation he felt or a combination of all three. Whatever it was he didn't want this moment to end. He felt safe.

"I'd really like to go to the anti-metric system rally today. We did promise Joseph and it's not that far from here." Barbara then took a sip of her coffee and looked at John with an anxious look that a child has asking their parents to take them to the amusement park.

John looked into her eyes and knew that he couldn't say no. He then thought that she is good and that she's going to get her way a lot. "Ok, we'll go to the rally. What time does it start?"

"It starts at noon."

John looked at a clock on the kitchen wall. "Well, it's twenty after eight right now. How far away is it from here?"

"About ten blocks away."

"So what are we going to do for the next three hours?"

Barbara got a devilish look on her face. John nodded.

...

As John walked with Barbara towards the rally he felt comfortable holding her hand in his. The weather was a beautiful sunny day, not too hot and not too cold. He felt like he should be saying something but realized that with her he didn't have to. He thought that Barbara enjoyed the silence. She was so comfortable with what was going on around her that she didn't need to tell him. John realized that he could learn a lot from her.

About five blocks away they started to hear the loud thunderous sound of people cheering and drums pounding. Each block they walked the sound was becoming deafening. As they turned onto Taggard Boulevard they saw how large the crowd was. "I don't believe it," John gasped. The entire downtown area was packed wall to wall with people. "Look at that, it goes on for at least ten blocks. I have never seen so many people in one place in my entire life."

"Just think, you'll be able to tell your grandchildren one day that you were here," Barbara said it with such casual way that it caught John off guard. His heart started to beat rapidly. He wasn't sure if she was just saying that as a common expression or if she was talking about their grandchildren one day.

"Hey you guys!" Candy had noticed John and Barbara and came running over to them. "Isn't this amazing!"

"It, it sure is." John was still reeling from looking at the large crowd. He then turned to look at Candy and noticed her shirt. She was wearing a very tight red shirt with the letters "oz" and a number three above it like if it was cubed. Her shirt was at least three times too small and made her rather amble bosom look even larger than it normally did. John realized that he was staring at her chest and quickly made eye contact with her, telling himself don't look down, don't look down...

"That's a cute shirt, Candy," Barbara commented. "What does it mean?"

"It's a play on words. Ou zee cube." Candy proudly announced. Barbara gently shook her head slightly raising her shoulders. "Ou zee cube, aren't you cute. Get it. Aren't you cute?"

Barbara gave a polite smile. "That's cute; did you come up with that all by yourself?"

"I sure did! Everyone has been giving me compliments all day. Especially the guys. You like my shirt, John?"

John was staring at Candy but wasn't listening; his mind was still telling him not to look at the shirt.

"What?" Her question jarred him from his trance.

"My shirt. Do you get the shirt?"

"Where's Joseph? Has he spoken yet?" John wanted to change the conversation, and he was hoping that Barbara wasn't noticing.

"No, not yet. He's all excited about the poem he wrote last night. He says it's one of his best. I'm on my way to see him. He got me a back stage pass. I am so excited!" Candy ran off towards the main stage.

"Did you see the shirt she was wearing?"

John got nervous. "Shirt? What shirt? Was she wearing a shirt? I didn't notice? What was she wearing? I didn't see, um, clothing, um..."

Barbara laughed. "It's ok. You would have to be blind not to see her breasts popping out of that shirt."

"Oh really? I didn't notice." John was still trying to play it off, but even he knew this was a lost cause.

"Since we are starting our relationship I should let you in on some ground rules. You can look, but you can't touch. Sound ok?"

John felt relieved that Barbara wasn't upset with him. "Ok, sounds good." He looked at her and gave her a kiss. "Right now you're all that I want to look at."

"Keep this up and I'm going to need an insulin shot," Barbara joked.

An announcer took the stage and grabbed the microphone. "How's everyone doing?" A crowd of almost twenty thousand people all cheered at once. "Who here hates the metric system?" A near deafening roar came from the crowd again. "I am honored to introduce our first speaker, Tom Cirtem, owner of Cirtem Tool Parts."

An older man in his early sixties came onto the stage while the crowd was applauding. "My father started Cirtem Tool Parts out of our family's garage in 1947. Over the years he worked to grow the company.

When I took over almost twenty years later after his untimely death, I continued in his vision of producing tool parts that are standard and normal. None of this garbage metric crap." The crowd cheered wildly. "For over sixty-five years we have not made a metric part and we never will." Tom had to raise his voice to a loud scream at the end of the sentence to keep up with the yelling from the crowd. He waited for moment to let the noise die down. He looked out in the audience with cold steel eyes, his body tense like a man possessed by a passion that he couldn't hold in. "We don't need metric tools, we don't need Celsius. We don't need the stinking metric system. And no civilized country needs it either."

Someone in the crowd waited for the cheering to die down and yelled at Tom. "What about Canada?" A whole bunch of people started to boo.

Tom got a stern look on his face. "Who was the coward who said that? Do you have courage to say that to my face?" No one took credit for the heckling. "If you think you know so much Mr. Metric Lover answer me this. Why is when someone goes to the doctor in Canada they don't weigh you in grams but in pounds. They don't measure you in centimeters, but in inches. Take a look at their stoves, they are in Fahrenheit. And the Canadian Football League, do they use meters to measure the field?" A loud NO erupted from the crowd. Tom decided to play to the crowd. "I don't hear you?" An even louder NO came from the crowd. "That's right they use yards, not meters, but yards like normal people would do." The crowd nearly exploded in excitement. Tom waved to the crowd and handed the microphone back to the emcee.

"Tom Cirtem, everyone. Visit his outlet store just up the block there on Taggard Boulevard and take the kids on the factory tour. As we're getting the effigy of Gabriel Mouton to burn, I want to introduce our next presenter. Many of you may have seen him at the Cafe Wombat rattling off some of his amazing poems. I've been told he wrote a new one just for today, and I can't wait to hear it. It is my honor to now bring Joseph Thompson, vice president of Poets Against the Metric System."

Barbara grabbed John's arm. "This should be exciting. I wonder what he wrote in such a short period of time." From where John and Barbara were standing Joseph looked like a small action figure on the large stage.

Joseph walked up on the stage with a folded piece of paper in his hand. On the side of the stage Candy was watching with her hands clenched tightly together up to her chin watching with pure excitement.

John turned to Barbara, "You know I am real proud of him. This is his shining moment and I'm really happy for him." John realized that he wasn't jealous but felt pride in knowing Joseph back when he wasn't known and had been his friend all those years. Just before Joseph spoke, John noticed something strange in the crowd. There were a number of people wearing trench coats and hats moving around in the crowd. He though one of them was wearing white makeup on his face but couldn't tell for sure. He looked back at Barbara. "Ever get the feeling that something bad is just about to happen?"

Joseph started to speak. "Thank you everyone. It is my honor to be here with you all today, my fellow brothers and sisters, to stand strong and fight the plague known as the metric system and keep it from ruining our lives. My poem is called The Metric System is the Tool of the Devil." Loud cheering came from the crowd. "Oh evil centimeter how you burn my home and--"

All of a sudden there was a loud explosion up the street. Flames shot out of Cirtem's factory and tool bits rained down on the street. A fireball rose to the sky and everything within a few feet of the factory caught on fire. People started to scream and run towards the front of the rally.

John noticed that the people running around suspiciously were mimes. They were no longer wearing their disguises. One of them had a tray of plastic water bottles with a rag stuck out of the top. Another mime was lighting the fuses and throwing the bottles. Since they were plastic they weren't breaking but bouncing off the shop windows and rolling around on the ground causing the gasoline to spill everywhere. It didn't take long until these pools of gasoline started to catch on fire creating even more panic. One of the mimes got caught on fire and started to run into the crowd. He was about to grab a small child when a man wearing a jacket with a red slash though a kilometer symbol on the back of his jacket intervened. He pulled the mime aside and threw him to the ground. A few other men wearing the same type of jacket came over and all of them started to put out the flames on the mime. The mime sat up and gave a pantomimed gesture for thank you. Then the men started to beat up on the mime mercilessly.

Another mime ran over to the ones lighting the Molotov cocktails and started to pantomime with great exaggeration expressing his anger. John was watching all of this in horror. There were more explosions from the gasoline burning under cars. Mobs of people were running in different directions, and he thought he heard some gun shots. All of a sudden a mime on a hang glider came floating about twenty feet above the crowd dropping fliers. They rained down on the crowd in a bizarre ticker tape parade. A group of mimes on the roof of the Helios building unfurled a large banner. It said IF GOD HAD WANTED US TO USE THE METRIC SYSTEM HE WOULD HAVE GIVEN US TEN FINGERS.

John picked up one of the fliers. The caption on the top read 'You Are Slaves To The Imperial Measurement System.' It attacked those who did not support the metric system. John gave it a quick glance and saw bullet points including asking 'Which is more? 2 quarts, 5 pints or 36 fluid ounces?' Another one was mocking the United States for being lumped in with Liberia and Burma as the only other countries not to take on the metric system, asking how many pounds in 200 ounces, which is larger 13/64, 1/4 or 5/32, how inane is it to not base temperature in a system where water doesn't freeze at zero degrees. The bottom had printed in large bold letters saying we can be proud to know that we are just like Napoleon Bonaparte who attempted to remove the metric system from France but was defeated and it came back in 1840 and the day will come here soon.

John dropped the flier and looked around for Barbara. She was in the crowd helping people who had fallen down to get up. She was helping them to the side to keep them from getting trampled. John heard police sirens and saw a few fire trucks pull up. A group of men wearing the red slash through the Km symbol were running through the crowd like salmon going up stream. John now remembered who they were, the were with the anti-metric system league, the same ones he saw in the bar last week with Joseph. They were carrying bats and chains and looking for anyone who looked like a mime. A mime was trying to run away and they started to beat him. Two police officers came over and pulled the mime out of the pile and put handcuffs on them. John thought that if it wasn't for the police that mime would be dead.

He ran over to Barbara. "Are you ok?" She nodded. "I think we need to get out of here."

"What about Joseph?" she asked.

"I think he's ok. He was up on stage and the fire started at the back of the rally."

"What about all these people here?" Barbara looked a bit panicked; something John was not familiar with seeing her do.

"The police are here. There are ambulances, fire department. We need to keep ourselves safe. You've done all you could."

Barbara looked around and saw the chaos and then looked at John. In a matter of a second she snapped back into her normal character and looked like she was back in control of the situation. "You're right. We need to go now," she responded calmly to John. She grabbed John's hand and pulled him with her as they ran down the street. They ran about a block and slowed down. People were still racing by them and police cars were going in the direction of the riot.

Chapter Eight

John arrived at work Monday morning still shaken up from what happened over the weekend. He stayed over with Barbara on Saturday to keep her calm, but he realized it was her keeping him calm. On Sunday evening he finally went home feeling numb from the weekend. The emotional highs and lows just wore him out. He also realized that he didn't like waking up alone and found himself really missing Barbara.

He was up late watching the news. They had arrested five mimes who were called the ringleaders of what was now being called the metric system riot. The death toll was up to seventeen people, with hundreds being treated for injuries ranging from bruises to third degree burns. The media said it was the second largest metric system massacre on record but far short of the forty people who died in Cleveland three years ago. Not much information was given about those arrested not their names or pictures of them.

John parked and while he was walking to the front door of the office, two police officers came up to him. They were dressed in regular clothes but there was a police car parked in the parking lot. They walked up to John.

"Sir, Are you John Warsley?" the police officer in a gray hat asked John.

"Yes I am." John responded.

"Don't play dumb with us." the other officer blurted out. Both John and the first police officer stared at him. "He knows what I mean. I'm watching you, dude."

"I'm Officer Grove, this here is Officer Forest", the police officer responded. "Do you know a William Agni?"

"Yeah, he works here." John replied.

"Have you seen him, buddy?" Officer Forest replied in an angry manner.

John looked a bit confused. "Have you tried looking inside?"

"He wasn't there." replied Officer Grove. "If you see him have him call me," he handed a business card to John, "It's regarding a factory fire last week just south of town." John thought for a second and got nervous.

"You know anything about a factory burning down?" Officer Forest looked at John with a suspicious look.

"No, only the one burned on Saturday," John answered in a somber tone.

Officer Grove nodded. "I know kid; it was tough on all of us. My nephew is out of a job right now. He'd been working there for six months."

"Lousy mimes," Officer Forest muttered. They both walked to the police car and drove off.

John walked into the office and saw Barbara who was on the phone. She waved to him, and he waved back. John walked into the technicians' area and saw William sitting at his desk. "You know the cops were looking for you? Did you see them?"

Without looking up from his computer William casually responded. "Nope, wasn't aware of it."

John walked over to his desk and saw a large greenish purple orb sitting in the middle of his desk. "What is this?"

"It's a purple guava," William responded.

"What's it doing here?"

"It's a gift from my uncle. They're grown in Brazil."

John thought for a moment. He picked up the guava and held it like a baseball. "You know the cops were asking me about a factory that burned down last week just south of town."

William looked up in a panic. "You didn't say

anything, did you?"

John was puzzled. "What would I say to them? Was that you're uncle's facto--"

"No, it wasn't," William interrupted John before he could finish his sentence. "Anyway, there's more of where those came from. I got a crate of them at home."

John sat down and noticed the television was on. There had been twenty-four hour news coverage since Saturday about the metric system event. He looked around and did not see Fred or Tim which made him feel better. Nothing new had been reported, but John watched the news broadcast anyway.

William looked at the television for a moment. "Such a tragedy. Were you there?"

"Yeah, it was pretty scary."

"My girlfriend has been in the police precinct since yesterday morning. She has been acting as a translator for the police with the mimes."

"Is your girlfriend a mime?" John asked.

"No she isn't. She did go to clown college so she knows how to communicate with them. If she had her choice she would like to see them fry for what they did."

A news logo came across the screen with the caption Metric System Massacre with a broken ruler and a crudely drawn mime holding a torch. "This is Action News channel nineteen, anchorman Ken Ruffington and there is breaking news in the Metric System Massacre. Police have released the names and photos of the five mimes arrested Saturday, known as the Silent Five."

The screen showed five individual photos of mimes. All looked the same with white face makeup and black and white horizontal striped shirts. The last photo had the name Mr. Bubbles aka Jacques Decroux. The newscaster spoke, "Here is the ringleader responsible for the massacre, Mr. Bubbles, whose real name is Jacques Decroux."

John recognized that mime as the one who made the threatening gesture towards him when he took Barbara out to dinner last week. "I've seen him before," John said to William. "He looked at me when I sat down in a restaurant and ran his finger across his throat as if suggesting he wanted to cut my throat."

"Action Nineteen News has learned that famed defense attorney; Herb Fenkel will be representing the Silent Five and is giving a press conference right now outside the county jail. On the scene is action news reporter, Jane Muharram."

"This is Jane Muharram outside the county jail with famed defense attorney, Herb Fenkel, who Action Nineteen News has just learned that he will be defending the Silent Five."

Ken Ruffington interrupted the reporter. "Jane, that has been covered already, the viewers know that."

"Well Ken, I was giving my introduction."

"Well Jane, we'd all like to hear what Herb Fenkel is saying."

"Fine, Ken." Jane was visibly angered and walked off camera.

The camera zoomed in on Herb. "And at this time I have nothing further to say. No comment, but I will be having a press conference later today at eleven thirty at Domingo's Bar and Grill, where Monday is all you can eat chili and sardines for only five dollars. Two drink minimum is required." He started to walk down the steps of the county jail when a reporter came running up to him.

"Mr. Fenkel, can you comment on the footage on the Internet that shows Mr. Bubbles was not at the rally on Saturday."

Herb stopped and looked at the reporter. "That's a very good question. All I can say at this time--".

The screen cut to a channel nineteen news logo. "We interrupt this program to annoy you and make your life miserable."

It then cut back to Herb Fenkel. "And that's all I can say about that until the trial. Thank you, no more questions until the press conference. Thank you."

Tim walked into the office. "How's everyone doing?" John and William looked at Tim and then turned back to the television. "What are you guys watching?"

"News coverage of the massacre." John didn't like using that word, but he couldn't think of anything else to call it."

"What massacre? What's going on?" Tim asked with confusion in his voice.

John sighed, "Nothing."

"Well then, I need for you to head over on a repair ticket this morning. It appears that Cirtem Tool's equipment went off line this weekend. So I'm going to need for you to look at that." John looked at Tim with an incredulous look or horror. "What?"

John was at a loss for words but somehow spit them out. "The factory is not there."

Tim was confused. "Are they closed on Monday?"

"No, the factory blew up on Saturday." John shook his head in disbelief. "During the metric system riot, the mimes blew up the factory and burned it to the ground."

Tim looked surprised. "It's the first I've heard of it."

William looked at Tim with a look of surprise. "Do you live in a cave?"

"No, I don't live in a cave. I just don't listen to the news."

"Well, the factory was blown up on Saturday,

94

seventeen people are dead and hundreds more were injured," John responded somberly.

"Hmm, sorry to hear that," Tim calmly said. "Well, can you head over there this morning?"

John put his right hand over his eyes and put his head down and rubbed his eyes. He looked up hoping that Tim would have disappeared, no such luck. "I can't head over there since there is no building. It was burned to the ground."

"I can head over," William piped up.

"Now there's a team player." Tim commented proudly.

William thought for a moment. "You know it may take me all day. I might need overtime for this."

"You do what you have to do, teammate," Tim turned to John. "You can learn a lot from William." He then turned and walked out of the technicians' area.

John looked at William. "You are not seriously going to take the day off?"

William chuckled. "Gotta do what the boss requests. See you tomorrow." As he walked out he yelled back to John. "And don't talk to the police."

John sat there staring at the television. He thought nothing new was going on. He didn't want to spend the day watching the same reports over and over again. Walking into the front area of the office he saw Barbara typing on the computer. When she saw him she stopped and looked at him lovingly. "Why don't you come over for dinner tonight?"

John thought about how miserable he was last night being alone and how having some company would take his mind off this malaise he was feeling. "Sounds good, thanks."

"It's common to feel depressed after such a horrible event. Find something that gives you happiness and peace."

"I thought that what I was doing now?" John smiled brightly.

"Very cute. What I mean is find your happiness through work," Barbara shot back.

"Are you now my boss?" John jokingly asked.

Barbara smiled. "Maybe I am."

Henry Jenkins walked in the door at that moment. He walked past Barbara and patted her on the head. "How's it going kid?" She smiled lovingly back at her father. "Tom, where are you?" He shouted.

Tim walked out of his office. "Did you call me, Mr. Jenkins?"

"Tom--"

"It's Tim sir."

"Right, whatever. I need men to carry in the new AE35 units on this truck in the parking lot. Where is everyone?" He looked at John. "Oh good, Tony is here."

"It's John, sir."

"Right, right. Sorry about that. I'm horrible with names, kid." He looked around the front office area. "Where is everyone else? Don't tell me that Fred is on the roof again? Where is that other guy, what's his name, Joey?"

Tim corrected him. "I think you're talking about William?"

"Yeah, where is that punk?"

"I sent him over on a repair ticket to the Cirtem factory."

Henry looked at Tim with a look of 'are you kidding me.' "Nice going idiot, you sent him to a burned out factory." He looked at his watch, sighed and shook his head. "Well, you two will need to bring these devices in. It'll take the two of you. Those things are pretty heavy." He looked at Tim. "You hear me?" Tim nodded. "Ok, time is a wasting. You help him, too,

James."

"John, sir."

"Right, John."

John walked outside to the parking lot with Tim. A truck was parked there that looked like it was driven from South America. The license plate was something that John had never seen before. John looked at Tim. "Why don't you climb up and bring down the first one and we'll see how hard it is to bring one."

Tim shook his head disapprovingly. "I got a better idea. Why don't you stay down here and I'll climb up into the truck."

John looked at Tim and thought that this could go on all day or he could just keep quiet and it will be over soon enough. "Great idea boss."

Tim felt satisfied with his accomplishment. He climbed up and attempted to pick one up. He failed. "These things are really heavy. I'm going to slide it to the edge and we'll pull it off together."

John was surprised at how well Tim had thought this out. Logic was not Tim's friend. It generally didn't acknowledge him and avoided him at all costs. They both lifted the box off the truck and slowly walked it over to the front door.

Henry was holding it open for them. "Good job boys, put some muscle into it."

They carried it to the storage room in the back of the office. and gently put it down. "One down, eleven more to go, huh?" John commented. Tim nodded in agreement, looking a bit winded from the experience. John noticed this. Normally he wouldn't care if this could have given Tim a heart attack, but his new found embrace of logic won John over. "Want to take a break?" Tim waved John off and walked back out to the truck.

After Tim slid the next unit over and they lifted it off

the truck, Tim's cell phone rang. John knew it was Tim's cell phone because it was the most annoying ring tone ever invented. Without thinking Tim grabbed for his phone letting go of the very heavy AE35 unit. John attempted to yell at Tim to not let go but before he could Tim had stepped aside and allowed the unit to drop on John's right leg. "Hello, hello? Nobody there. John, what are you doing down there?"

John was lying on the ground experiencing the most pain he had ever felt in his entire life. He tried to yell out in pain but he felt like he was short of breath. He looked up at Tim who stood over him confused. "Come on John, get up. Walk it off." John though that if he could stand up at this very moment he would strangle Tim.

Henry came running out after watching it from inside the office. "Great, this will kill my insurance." He looked at Tim "What's next, genius, you're going to set the building on fire?"

Barbara came running out with a jacket and put it under John's head. "I've already called for an ambulance. They should be here in about a minute." She caressed John's hair and kissed his forehead. Its ok, you'll be at the hospital in a few minutes. I'm not going anywhere." John grabbed her hand and winced in pain. He felt himself getting tired. He looked up and as his eyes were closing he saw Fred staring at him from the roof of the building.

...

"Sir, sir. You cannot smoke a cigar in the hospital." The nurse firmly spoke.

John opened his eyes and looked around. He realized that he was in a hospital room.

Henry Jenkins closed his Zippo lighter with a single

flick of his wrist giving the nurse a threatening stare. The nurse walked out of the room and shut the door. Henry promptly lit his cigar. He looked over and saw John with his eyes open. "Good, he's alive."

John stared at Henry trying to get his bearings straight. He noticed his right leg was bandaged up and was in a sling elevating it above his body. Barbara came over and gave him a gentle kiss on his forehead. "Where am I?" he groggily asked.

"We're in Shanghai-La, kid," Henry said with deep sarcasm out of the side of his mouth since he was chomping down on his cigar. "Were do you think we are? We're in a hospital."

John smiled. "Probably could have guessed that. You don't look much like Ronald Colman."

Henry gave a hearty laugh. "I like this kid. I see why you're dating him," he said to Barbara.

John shot a surprised glance at Barbara. She stroked his head. "I had to tell him because he got suspicious when I was being nice to one his employees." John looked at her and realized that she was making a joke.

"All right kid," Henry said while chomping on his cigar, "you're not going to sue the company?"

John looked at Henry with surprise. "Why would I sue the company?"

Henry gave a nervous laugh. "Of course, you won't kid. Still will need you to sign something to that effect."

John sat up and rested on his elbows and looked Henry squarely in the eyes. "I'm not signing anything. I said I won't be suing. I give you my word and that's all you get. You don't like it, too bad." John said with firm authority.

Henry walked over to the bed and leaned in over John. He accidentally let out a puff of cigar smoke into

John's face. "Sorry about that kid."

John gave a slight cough as he turned his head to the side and waved off the smoke. "It's all right, don't worry about it."

"I like you kid. I should promote you to management." John liked the sound of that. To be in charge, he thought. He could fire everyone especially Tim. Well, not everyone, he would have to keep Barbara. "Hey, are you still with me here kid?"

John realized that he was daydreaming and wasn't paying attention to Henry. "I'm sorry, what did you say?"

Henry repeated himself, "I asked, do you remember what happened?"

John thought back for a moment and replayed the entire incident in his head. He and Tim were holding the device, Tim's cell phone rang and Tim let go of the device causing it drop on John's foot. "All I remember is that the device slipped out of Tim's hands and fell on my foot."

"Is that what really happened?" Henry asked with a hint of doubt in his voice.

John looked up at Henry. He knew that blaming Tim wasn't going to accomplish anything. He would get his revenge on Tim soon enough. He also didn't get by as he had in his career by being a cry baby and blaming other people. "Yes, that is what happened. Tim was a bit tired after carrying the first one and it must have slipped out of his hands by accident."

Henry nodded his head slowly and looked at John. John felt uneasy and tense. He hated to lie, but he was developing a much bigger goal right now and didn't want anything to derail him from the start. In John's mind it felt like Henry was staring at him for minutes. Finally he spoke. "Ok, we'll leave it at that. You get better kid." He patted John on the shoulder.

"I'm covering the hospital stay and I'll get you on some desk duty for a while to let you heal." He looked at Barbara. "Is there enough paperwork to keep him busy?" She nodded her head. "Good." He walked over to Barbara and gave her a kiss on the forehead. "Take care of him." She nodded and gave her father a hug. Henry walked out of the room.

Albert opened the door and stuck his head in. "Everyone from the office is here and wanted to check in on you. Is it ok to come in?" John nodded and waved for Albert to come in.

Albert was followed by William, Fred and Tim. William walked over to the bed. "So what's the damage buddy?"

John shrugged. "Don't know, I just woke up. Not in any pain though."

"The doctor said it was a broken fibula, but it was a clean break." Barbara answered.

William chuckled. "Guess you won't be climbing any ladders any time soon." John laughed.

Tim decided to chime in. "That's part of his rehab." No one laughed and everyone looked at Tim with disgust. Tim looked at John who gave him an angry cold stare and quickly averted his eyes to the ground.

Fred walked over. "I just want you to know that even though there has been a lot of controversy, I support you in your desire to get a sex change operation and become a man."

John shook his head in disbelief. "I'm not getting a sex change, I'm already...look I can't even begin to deal with you. Please go away from me. Go stand by the door." Fred followed John's orders as if he was a zombie under his command. John thought he may need to take advantage of this and do this more often.

John didn't notice it when they walked in, but Albert had brought in with him a large old style boom box.

He pulled a cassette tape from his shirt pocket. "John, since you've seen the movie I wanted you to hear the opening theme to the movie. It wasn't ready for the showing but I will be adding it in post-production." He put the cassette tape into the radio and pressed play. A loud thumping sound came from the speakers that filled the room so that nothing else could be heard.

John covered his ears. He thought that it was the worst sounding music, if you could call it that, he had ever heard in his life. "Could you please turn it off?" he shouted at Albert.

Albert looked at John confused. "What?"

John tried a second time to convey his message. "I said could you turn that off."

Albert nodded. "Last Tuesday."

"No, I don't want to know when it was made!" John yelled in vain.

"DJ Schmaltz. I agree, he is good."

John was losing his patience. "Just turn it off!"

"Sure, I can make it louder." Albert turned up the volume to the maximum level and started to dance to the music.

John lay in the hospital bed thinking that Albert just made the list. He looked around the room. Tim was avoiding eye contact and looking nervously at the chairs and walls. Fred was still standing by the open door just staring at John. William was outside in the hallway trying to hit on a nurse. Barbara came back in with the doctor following her.

The doctor looked at John's leg and nodded. "Looks like it's broken." He turned around and started to walk out of the room.

At that moment Albert's tape jammed and the cassette exploded out of the radio. John used the moment of silence to call out to the doctor. "Excuse me, doctor?" He turned back to look at John. "Can you offer anything more than it's broken?"

The doctor looked at John. "Nope." He started to walk away again.

"Look doctor, I don't mean to be a bother--"

"Look I have a hospital full of burn victims, people who were trampled and what angers me the most is three of those disgusting mimes are under police protection. And I have to treat them! I'm about ready to let the mob come in and beat them to death. Lord knows they deserve it." The doctor was seething at this point.

"Doctor, I'm sorry. It must be very difficult," John said politely.

The doctor sighed and put his head down. "No, I'm sorry. I haven't got much sleep since Saturday. You seem like a good guy. I'll go tell the nurse to give you some extra morphine." He walked outside the room and John could see through the window the doctor talking to the same nurse that William was talking to. William was getting visibly annoyed about the doctor interrupting his conversation and started to yell at the doctor. The doctor punched William in the face and William fell to the ground.

A few seconds later a nurse walked in and she injected something into John's arm. Almost immediately John started to feel calm and relaxed. The nurse looked around the room. "Everyone who is not family will need to leave." She turned to Barbara. "You can stay with your husband." Barbara was caught off guard and blushed.

John's voice was now slurred as he looked at the nurse. "She's not my wife. Not yet that is." John then fell into a deep sleep.

The next thing John knew he was driving an green van with speakers on the top of the vehicle. He wasn't holding the steering wheel, but the van was swerving back and forth across a two lane road. All of a sudden he slammed on the brakes and saw that there was a tree planted in the middle of the road. He got out of the van and walked up to the tree. It appeared to have been there for a long time.

He started to walk down the road past the tree. He came upon a man who had a bucket on his head with a frown drawn on the front of it. A group of women dressed as angels came skipping by and started to throw tennis balls at the bucket until the man fell over. One of the angels turned to John, "Mango juice packs a punch." She then skipped off with the other angels.

John turned around and his great uncle Irving was standing right there. "Wake up, John; you're having a bad dream." John realized that this was a dream. He all of a sudden sat up and he was in his Uncle Irving's apartment where he was sleeping on the couch. "John, it's a good thing I told you to wake up." John rubbed his eyes and nodded in agreement. "You're awake?" his uncle asked John. John shook his head yes, but noticed that he couldn't open his mouth. It felt really dry and he couldn't feel his tongue. "Don't talk, John. I have something very important to tell you." John looked at his uncle attentively. "You need to stop Pol Pot from going to New Hyde Park." John gave a confused look to his uncle. "If he gets there he will change all cities, roads and words to New Hyde Park."

John blinked and found himself standing on a street corner and the street signs said New Hyde Park Road and the cross street was New Hyde Park Avenue. All the signs in the window said New Hyde Park. Someone walked by and waved hello, "New Hyde Park" they said and kept on walking. John turned and saw his uncle walk out of a butcher shop. "I warned you," his uncle told him, "I warned you we needed to stop this." John realized that he still couldn't talk. He started to panic. His uncle came over and put his arm around him. "Don't worry, my boy, I'll buy you a knish."

They walked on the sidewalk which then turned into sand and then back to a wood floor. His uncle walked over to a hot dog vendor. "New Hyde Park, New Hyde Park, hablah, alacazam, New Hyde Park." The vendor nodded and handed his uncle Irving two very large knishes. His uncle walked back and handed him a knish. "I think we're safe, the language has begun to mutate."

John opened his eyes. He head was turned to his left side looking at the outside window in the room. His mouth was all dry. He heard muffled chanting from the street. He couldn't make it out but it sounded like kill the mimes or something to that effect. He rolled his head over hoping to see Barbara but Fred was sitting in a chair staring at John. He was eating a Styrofoam cup. John closed his eyes and went back to sleep.

Chapter Nine

John recovered much quicker than he thought he would. The first few days were the toughest, but after a while he didn't need crutches and walked with a cane. As soon as he didn't need to have his leg elevated all the time he went back to work. He found being white collar was much nicer than doing physical labor. There was a never ending supply of work that Barbara gave John, but he was keeping up and learning about the business.

This was working well into his goal of rising in management and being able to get rid of those he didn't like which was almost everyone who worked there. Barbara had taken care of John. First, by staying at his apartment helping him until he could walk again. When he was ready to go back to work she had him stay at her place since John was unable to drive and because she wanted to take care of him. She made him lunch every day and would baby him when they were at home. By the time John could drive again they would split living at John's apartment on the weekend and Barbara's apartment during the week since it was closer to work.

John had no trouble with the rest of the staff in his new role. He rarely had to work with Albert unless he needed data for a report. William treated John as his supervisor since he hated Tim so much and thought it would annoy him. Fred was a zombie that followed John's orders. Tim avoided John. He realized that John didn't openly blame him for the injury and was scared that revenge would be coming soon. Tim found ways to work without being noticed. He now started to avoid Henry Jenkins as well. This worked for Henry since he never liked Tim and would find ways of trying to avoid him too. Since Tim was taking care of that for him, Henry started showing up at the office a bit more often. John was satisfied with this situation since he wanted to become a manager and he wanted to show Henry that he had managerial qualities. John started to get know Henry and try to become his friend. He would run errands for Henry, get him cigars as gifts, answer his emails, and other tasks making him an admin assistant.

Deep down John was starting to realize that he wanted Barbara to be his wife. He felt that if he could win over Henry then he would feel comfortable asking Barbara. He was thinking about buying an engagement ring. He knew she was the one and he knew that she would accept, but he didn't know how to buy jewelry and wanted to get something nice but affordable.

One afternoon while out running some errands for the office John drove by Simon Family Jewelers and decided he will buy that ring today. He walked in and there was a woman behind a display counter. "How are you today, sir?"

John smiled. "I'm doing well."

"Are you?" the woman asked John.

John was a bit confused. "Yes, yes I am."

"Very good sir. How may I help you? My name is Barbara."

John's eyes lit up. "What wonderful luck. I'm here to buy an engagement ring for my girlfriend and her name is Barbara."

"Did I say Barbara? I'm sorry my name is Jane."

"Then why did you say your name was Barbara?"

"Very good sir. So what kind of ring were you thinking of buying?"

John got a sheepish look on his face. "I don't know. I'm not good with jewelry, but I want to get her something nice but affordable. Can you recommend something?"

"How about a watch?"

"Why would I give a watch to my girlfriend if I want to ask her to marry me? I want to give her an engagement ring."

"You don't like watches?"

"Of course I do-- what does that have to do with this?"

"How about you sign up for a store credit card and I can offer you a free battery change on the watch?"

"First off, why would I need to change the battery on a new watch, and secondly I don't want a watch I want an engagement ring."

"Very good, sir, then. How about a watch and a ring?"

"No, I don't want a watch I just want a ring."

"So just a watch then?"

John rubbed his forehead in frustration. When he finally left two hours later he got a ring that he knew Barbara would love. Now he just had to find a good place to hide it since Barbara was now staying over every weekend.

John held off asking Barbara because he wanted to wait for the perfect moment. This went on for months. A few times he thought would be right, but he could never get the nerve to ask her. He knew the right moment would come, he hoped.

One day John was in Henry's office fixing his computer. Henry didn't like computers and would usually create some sort of mess that he couldn't figure out. Unlike Tim who usually made the problem worse, John could fix these simple mistakes. Just before John was going to walk out of Henry's office, Henry pulled his cigar out of his mouth.

"Jack, I want to ask you something."

"It's John, sir."

"Right, right, John. Sorry about that. I am getting better."

"Yes Henry, you are," John replied with a smile.

"When are you going to ask my daughter to marry you?"

John looked at Henry with guilty surprise, like a child who gets caught with his hand in the cookie jar by his parents. "What makes you say, I never said, did I, um marry Barbara?"

"John, I'm old but I'm not blind. The two of you love each other. You've already bought an engagement ring. Why not pop the question?"

John was now very surprised. He thought how did Henry know I bought a ring? Does he have a network amongst the jewelers? How far does his reach go? Or has he been having me followed? "How did you know I bought an engagement ring?"

Henry laughed. "I didn't until I just saw the look on your face. Seriously, my boy, you need to learn how not to reveal what you are thinking. It's called a poker face." John looked at the ground sheepishly. "So what are you waiting for? My approval?"

John was trying to find the right words. He had practiced this speech hundreds of times of what he would say to Henry. But all he could do was quietly mumble, "Yes sir."

Henry gave John a sly look and then lit up his cigar. "Ok, my boy, you got my approval. Now go squeeze the trigger and ask her before she finds someone better." John stood frozen solid looking at Henry trying to absorb what had just happened. "Go on boy, you're dismissed." Henry said with a big smile.

John walked out of Henry's office and grabbed his chest. His heart was beating a mile a minute. That felt like the most terrifying event in his life. After a few moments he realized what happened, he can now ask

Barbara to marry him. He knew Henry was right; don't put off to tomorrow what you have to do today. John then thought Henry didn't say that, but if that is what he got from it that is all though should matter. John now realized that he is over analyzing this and needed to talk to Barbara.

As John walked towards Barbara's desk he started to think what excuse he could use to go back to his place and get the ring. He approached her desk and she looked up at him with a smile. "I just remembered that I am running out of mouthwash at your place. Let me borrow the car and I'll head over now while it's quiet and get what I have left at my apartment."

Barbara looked at John quizzically. "We can stop off and pick some up at the store on the way home."

"Sure, but I have a bottle already open in my bathroom that I can just easily grab."

"Isn't that the bottle you brought over to my place?"

"I mean that I have another bottle at my place." The phone rang and Barbara picked it up. John stared at her with the puppy dog look that she had perfected and used on him many times before. Barbara rolled her eyes, reached into her purse and handed John her keys. "Thank you." Barbara waved back at him with her free hand.

John raced back to his apartment and took the ring out of the hiding place he had under a bottom drawer in his desk. He then raced back to work so that Barbara wouldn't get suspicious. He walked in the office and gave Barbara back her keys.

"Did you get your mouthwash?" Barbara asked.

John panicked. He forgot to get mouthwash to cover his lie. "It's in the car. Say you want to go out tonight and try that new barbeque place downtown?"

"Sure," Barbara calmly responded. John looked at Barbara. She was looking at the computer screen and typing something. John believed that he may have got away with his story and if all goes well tonight he thought he will be engaged.

....

John pulled up in front of what he thought was the barbeque restaurant. There were no signs, but one store had black smoke seeping out from under the door. He parked and walked with Barbara to the store and opened the door. A big cloud of black smoke came bursting out of the restaurant. Two waiters were standing inside but didn't see John and Barbara enter.

"So since I was in a hurry this morning, I grabbed my work pants and wore them to my class. Everyone except for two people asked me if my house burned down," the first waiter said.

"You should have told them, 'Yeah, it did and you know what, yours might be next,'" the second waiter said jokingly. He turned around and saw that John and Barbara were waiting in the lobby. He immediately attended to them. "Yes sir, two for dinner?" John nodded. "Please come this way." As they followed the waiter he grabbed a handful of towels, barbeque tongs and oven mitts. He led them into the restaurant.

Each table had a barbeque grill built into it. On the side was a bucket full of charcoal briquettes and a bucket of barbeque sauce. People were grilling large chunks of beef on the grills, there did not appear to be any ventilation. The room was thick and heavy with smoke. The waiter sat John and Barbara. "Here are your utensils, the charcoal is in this bucket on the left and the barbeque sauce is the one on the right. You don't want to mix them up."

John looked at the waiter and noticed that his eyes

were red and bloodshot. "So we have to cook our dinner ourselves?"

"Yes sir. We are a do it yourself barbeque restaurant. I can bring you a menu of the slabs that we have tonight." The waiter turned and walked away.

John looked around and saw that there was a thick black cloud of smoke above the room. People were cooking large chunks of meat. The room felt like it was about one hundred and five degrees. On a positive note the aroma was amazing.

John looked at Barbara and decided this was the right moment. "Barbara I want to--"

"Here is our tonight's menu." The waiter wheeled in a tray of beef. "What would you like?"

John was shaken by the distraction. "What?"

"Tonight's menu sir. What would you like?"

"I don't care." John looked at the tray of raw beef. "I'll take some ribs." The waiter grabbed a handful of ribs with his bare hand and dropped them on the table. He then walked back into the kitchen. John looked back at Barbara. "Where was I? Oh yes. Barbara since we started dating I've--". Barbara pointed to the television that was behind John.

The television on the wall was interrupted by a news bulletin. "This is Action Nineteen News with breaking news about the Metric System Massacre. From our Action newsroom here's reporter, Tom Harkingstonson." The television cut to a man sitting at a newsroom desk. "This is Tom Harkingstonson with breaking news about what is being called the trial of the decade. We have word that closing arguments have just finished in the trial against the Silent Five, the mimes who are being held responsible for the Metric System Massacre. We have with us in the studio Igor Tobar News Nineteen's trial expert and we have live at the courthouse Action News Nineteen reporter Judy Pomgant. Judy, what can you tell us?"

The television cut to a woman wearing a large Carmen Miranda hat full of fruit. "Thanks, Tom, this is Judy Pomgant live at county courthouse and I have heard that the judge is now giving the jury their instructions. As you know this trial has gone on for over eight weeks and has had hundreds of witnesses, experts and has brought us great ratings."

The television cut back to Tom. "Say, Judy, that's a nice hat you're wearing. Is that a fashion statement?"

The television cut back to Judy who was in the process of taking the hat off. "No, Tom, this is a fundraiser for Timmy Thompson disease. Every time I wear this hat on television Earl's Pet Rock Funeral Parlor will donate five hundred dollars to the Timmy Thompson charity."

The television cut back to the studio. "Igor, what do you think will happen next?"

"Well, Tom," Igor thought for a second, "in my professional opinion I think they could be deliberating for weeks, maybe months."

"Judy, do you have an opinion you would like to offer?"

The television cut to Judy. In the background the jury was walking out of the courtroom. "Actually, I would like to complain about the parking here at the courthouse....wait a moment Tom, I just got word that the jury is coming back into the courtroom. Yes, they are taking their seats."

"Well, they must be requesting additional information," Igor commented.

Judy was turned to her left talking to someone off camera. "Yes, we can? Thank you. Tom, I just got word that we will be allowed to bring our cameras into the courtroom to bring you the jury's decision. It appears that the jury has come to a decision already.

We will now go live with Action News Nineteen coverage."

Tom interrupted, "Judy, that's Action Nineteen News, not Action News Nineteen."

The television cut back to Judy who was visibly annoyed, "Oh Tom, grow up."

The camera then cut to the judge. "Has the jury reached a verdict?" The foreman nodded. "Will the defendant rise?" Camera cut over to Mr. Bubbles dressed in a black and white horizontal striped shirt, black beret and white makeup on his face that had a frown drawn on it that stood up. "Will the jury read the verdict?"

The foreman spoke, "We, the jury, find the defendant guilty on all charges." A large cheer of approval came from the courtroom as well from the viewers in the restaurant. The judge banged his gavel and called for order which did not quiet down the crowd one bit. Inside the restaurant people were cheering wildly and high-fiving one another.

When the cheering died down a man wearing a blue coat and sitting near John spoke, "What do you expect; you knew that none of them would get a fair trial?"

A man wearing a baseball cap at another table responded, "What are you talking about? It was an open and shut case. You would have to be insane to think that filthy mime was innocent."

The man in the blue coat yelled back, "At least I don't have metamfiezomaiophobia."

The man in the baseball cap snapped back angrily, "How dare you claim I have a fear of mimes, pantomime or people in disguises. Sounds like to me you are a phronemophobiac."

The man in the blue coat became very angry. "Just because I don't agree with you, you accuse me of having a fear of thinking?"

Another man in the restaurant stood up trying to get the two men to stop fighting. "Gentlemen, let's be civilized here."

"Who asked the guy with amfisbitophobia to butt in?" The man in the blue coat responded sarcastically.

The man who stood up snapped back at the man in the blue coat. "I don't have a fear of arguing. Although looking at your face I am developing cacophobia."

The man in the blue coat laughed. "So you think I'm ugly, good." He then picked up his towel and yelled at the man in the baseball cap. "Hey, stupid, I hope you don't have petsetaphobia." He then threw the towel and it hit him right in the face.

The man in the baseball cap grabbed the towel angrily. "No, I don't have a fear of being hit by a towel. Hope you don't have carnophobia." He then picked up a chunk of raw meat and threw it back at the man in the blue coat, hitting him square on the nose.

The man in the blue coat wiped his face off. "If I had a fear of meat, would I be eating here in this restaurant, idiot?" He then walked over to the table of the man in the baseball cap with his table's bottle of lighter fluid and squeezed it on the table and then dropped a match on it. "Hope you don't have arsonphobia?"

The man in the baseball cap jumped up out of his seat. "Pyrophobia is the fear of fire, you jerk." He then grabbed the man in the blue coat and they wrestled to the ground. Their fight caused the table to fall over and the fire began to spread throughout the restaurant. People started to get up and run out.

Barbara looked at John. "We've got to get out of here now!" She jumped up out of her chair and grabbed John and they ran to the door.

At that moment the fire sprinklers on the ceiling

kicked in. The smell of French fries filled the air. In a few seconds the fluid from the sprinkler started to catch fire. The first waiter looked at the second waiter. "Why did you put the oil from the deep fryer in the sprinkler system?"

The second waiter shrugged his shoulders. "You told me to get rid of the oil and that I couldn't pour it down the sink."

By the time John and Barbara got outside the fire department was arriving. The two men fighting where now wrestling on the sidewalk outside the burning restaurant. People were gathering around them. Firemen were trying to hook up hoses and move people away from the fire. The fire was beginning to spread to the surrounding buildings.

John realized that it was now or never. He grabbed Barbara's hand. "Barbara, will you marry me?"

A fireman stopped his hose and looked at John. "Hey buddy, you got to get down on one knee."

John turned back to the fireman. "Shut up. Go put out the fire." The fireman shrugged and went back to fighting the fire. Everyone started to look at John and Barbara and stopped watching the fight. The two men fighting stopped to watch as well. John ignored all of them. He put the engagement ring on Barbara's finger.

Barbara looked down at the ring and gasped with excitement. She looked up at John. "Yes, yes I will." She kissed John and they hugged. The crowd began to cheer and whistle joining in the moment. While they were celebrating the fire continued to spread to the neighboring buildings and caused them to burn to the ground as well.

Chapter Ten

John let Barbara make all the decisions for the wedding. He figured it was better that way. All he had to do was show up and not forget his vows. Beyond that he didn't care. Barbara would show him things every now and then and he would tell her it was fine and that he trusted her tastes.

One morning Albert approached John at the office. "I would love to be the DJ at your wedding."

John started at Albert blankly, "No."

"Oh, come on, John. I promise it will be respectful." Albert was beginning to beg at this point. John thought for a second. "You can play during the reception not at the wedding. If you play anything at the wedding, I will kill you."

"You don't want Lohengrin, act three, part one by Wagner played?"

"What?" John looked at Albert with confusion.

"Here comes the bride?" Albert responded.

John nodded. "Ok, just that. Anything by DJ Schmaltz or other garbage, I promise I will kill you."

Albert nodded in agreement. "Seems fair enough to me."

The only other person from work who ended up getting an invite was William who said his uncle could provide a banquet hall for them free of charge. John was skeptical, but William took him and Barbara to the location and John liked it. Barbara said it was perfect. William bargained that this earned him an invite to the wedding which John and Barbara agreed was fair enough.

The wedding was a simple affair. There were about forty people in attendance, only family and close friends. Joseph was John's best man and his family sat in as John's family for the wedding. It was a happy occasion, no chaos, nothing to stress John. He was glad everything went well. He thought Barbara looked beautiful. The whole event went off as planned and everyone had a great time.

After the wedding John was sitting with a glass of scotch. Henry sat down next to John. "Nice wedding, kid."

John looked over to his right where Henry sat down to him. "Thank you, sir, I'm glad you were here today."

Henry reached into his coat pocket and pulled out a cigar and offered it to John. John thought for a moment and then took the cigar. Henry handed John a cigar cutter. John trimmed the end of his cigar and handed it back to Henry who followed suit. Henry pulled out a lighter and leaned over and lit John's cigar and then lit his. They sat there puffing away silently for a few minutes. After a while Henry broke the silence. "You know, kid, I like you. You remind me a lot of myself when I was your age."

"Thank you," John responded. "You know, I really like this cigar. I could easily develop a taste for these things. How long have you been smoking them?" John took another puff of his cigar.

Henry thought for a moment, "About thirty years. My father-in-law sent me a box of them when Barbara was born. Been smoking them ever since." Henry took a deep drag off his cigar.

"Henry, I want to ask you a favor."

"Go ahead kid."

"I would like for you to promote me to vice president of operations."

Henry took the cigar out of his mouth and looked in front of him. "Makes sense, you're pretty much doing the job already, everyone listens to you, and it might push that idiot Todd over the edge to quit."

"Do you mean Tim?"

118

"Right, whatever his name is. Can't stand him. That was the worst mistake I've ever made in business. That's what I get for listening to my wife." Henry put his cigar back into his mouth.

John was surprised. Henry never talked about his late wife. John thought that Henry might be the most relaxed that he had ever seen him. "Did your wife know Tim?"

"No, she didn't, but she suggested that I should hire him and I did. Two days later she died in a car accident. I always felt that since it was her last wish I couldn't bring myself to fire him." Henry turned to John. "Consider it done kid. I'll let everyone know while you two are on your honeymoon."

"Thanks Henry, I appreciate it."

John and Henry sat silently watching the wedding reception. At the far end of the banquet hall Fred was standing there staring at Henry and John. Henry leaned over to John. "Why did you invite Fred?"

John leaned over to Henry, "I didn't."

"You know, that guy scares me sometimes." Henry commented.

...

When John came back to work after his honeymoon, he had a new focus on his job. For the first time in years he looked forward to coming to work. He had spent a lot of time during his honeymoon planning out how to get rid of everyone. At times Barbara would catch him making notes and would get annoyed at him. John eventually started making mental notes to avoid any conflicts with Barbara.

First, he would establish new policies. Then each employee would be required to document their job description. John thought that this will help him when he had to place a help wanted ad to fill the positions. He figured that as they failed to meet the new criteria that he will have established, he could fire them. He couldn't wait to get to the office so he could get his notes ready for the staff meeting that he was going to call that morning.

John sat down at his desk and wondered why he was still sitting in the technicians' area? He thought that later today, he would move Tim out of his office and start using that as his own office. John wrote out an email and sent it to everyone in the office informing them of a meeting this morning at nine thirty. He sat back in his chair and smiled. Months of planning and hard work had led him to this day, to this point in time. And he was going to enjoy every second of it.

John started the meeting at nine thirty sharp. Everyone who worked for the company, with the exception of Henry, was all sitting in the technician area. "I want to thank everyone for coming to the staff meeting this morning. I'm sure you all know that I was promoted to vice president of operations." John looked around the room. Barbara was smiling at John. Albert nodded. William was looking something up on the Internet. Tim had a nervous look on his face and looked at the ground when John made eye contact with him. Fred was staring up at the ceiling with his mouth wide open. William looked up from his computer. "We know, John, that's great news. Are we done?"

John looked at William. "No, we are not done. As vice president I report directly to the owner of the company. This means the buck stops with me when Henry is not here." John added a pause to allow that to sink in with everyone. "So I want to tell you about the changes that will be happening starting--".

At this moment Henry walked into the technicians'

room with two strangely dressed men. The first was a large man, at least six foot two and four hundred pounds. He was dressed in what a noble would wear three hundred years ago. He was wearing a purple tri-corner hat with a powdered white wig underneath, an orange and blue striped silk vest that was so small for him that it could barely button. The buttons looked like they would shoot off at any moment. His pants were britches that cut off just above the knee. They were the same orange blue striping as the vest. And he had on white hosiery and buckle shoes. The other man was a short thin man, no taller than five feet. He was dressed in a Victorian era outfit that was three times too big for him. He was wearing a black bowler hat, a red and yellow polka dotted bow tie and a long black coat that in the back went down to his heels. He had tight vertical black and white pinstriped pants on and was wearing a pair of red sneakers and carrying a walking stick.

Everyone had stopped paying attention to John and had turned to stare at the two men with Henry. "I want to introduce you to these two gentlemen here." He pointed to the large man in the bizarre nobility costume. "This here is Blowgun."

The man stepped forward, clicked his heels and bowed. "Moeto ime e Blagun Kudline."

Henry looked at him strangely. "Very good. And this is his associate Zipper."

The short man took off his hat. "Zhelyazko Lyuben na golemiya grad Haskovo."

Henry continued. "These two fine men are the new owners of Jenkins Electrical." The room became dead silent. "I have sold them the company and will now be retiring."

John felt like someone had punched him in the gut. He looked around the room to get the reactions of everyone else. Albert was holding his hands out like he was framing a camera shot making a rectangle with his hands. William was eying the short guy looking like he was ready to go over and start a fight with him. Tim had a pleased look on his face like he was given a surprise Christmas gift. Fred was lying down face first on the floor not moving. Barbara had a look of furious anger on her face. She stared at Henry and just pointed with her right hand to his office.

Henry looked at Barbara and got a worried look on his face. "I'm going to be busy for a few minutes. Why don't you guys get to know your new bosses?"

William smirked. "Do they even know English?"

Henry was caught off guard. "Of course they do. Right, Zipper?"

Zipper's eyes lit up. "Applesauce."

"See, you're half way there." Barbara's look had grown fiercer. "I think I have to go talk to my daughter." Henry walked out of the technicians' room and walked to his office and went inside. Barbara followed behind him and slammed the door.

Everyone stood there staring at Blowgun and Zipper. Blowgun leaned down and whispered something to Zipper. He acknowledged and took a step forward and removed his hat. "Pozvolete mi da vi presdtavim Blagun Kudline, potomuk na Shishman Vidin dinastiya."

Blowgun bowed his head and clasped his hands as if he was saying a prayer. He looked up with a huge grin on his face. "Tova e vseizgaryane den kartofi. Yadosaniyat burkachka e dalech. No nie shte produlzhim nashata lilavo pistoleta gotov za bitkata na katerichkite, koito se opitvat i da pie kruvta mi." Zipper started to get tears in his eyes and began to applaud. Everyone was confused except for Albert who was holding up his phone, recording Blowgun's speech.

William spoke first, "So what do we do now?"

John shook his head disapprovingly, "I don't know."

Tim had a pleased look on his face. "Well, John, just a few minutes ago you said that the buck stops with you. You report to the owner of the company. Well, they are the new owners." For the first time in months Tim made eye contact with John, enjoying the misery that he would have dealing with the new owners.

The door to Henry's office opened. Barbara walked out calm. She wasn't smiling, but she no longer had the look of wanting to punch a hole in the wall on her face any more. It was surprisingly focused and relaxed. She sat down at her computer and started to type as if nothing was wrong.

Henry walked out and stood looking at Barbara. John walked over to him and just looked at him. Henry put his hand on John's shoulder. "Kid, I can't explain now, but this is for the best. You'll understand one day."

John gently removed Henry's hand from his shoulder and shook his head. "No, Henry, I don't think so." Henry nodded and gave one last look at Barbara. She didn't look at him, she was busy typing as if she didn't know he was there. Henry turned and walked out of the office.

John waited until Henry drove off and looked at Barbara. "Are you ok?" She nodded. "Do you want to talk about it?" She shook her head. "If you need anything?" She gave a nod of understanding. "Ok, I'll be here." She stopped typing for a second, sighed and then began typing again.

John walked back to his desk. In the midst of all of the chaos that just happened he forgot all about Barbara's plans for the company. He realized that she must be furious and feel cheated. John knew he was upset but he couldn't imagine how Barbara must be feeling. He thought that there has to be a way to fix this.

John sat at his desk. Tim had already gone back to his office. William had snuck out while John went to talk to Henry. Fred was nowhere to be found. Blowgun and Zipper were walking around the technicians' area taking inventory. Blowgun would pick up an item, give a long detailed speech and Zipper would scribble down detail notes. First, he picked up a paper clip, then an empty soda can, a Phillips head screwdriver and so on. Each item surprised him and he acted like he had never seen it before. John watched this and thought that unless there is some major cultural difference, all of these items are standard things that are common around the world. Their actions were somewhat comical, but he felt certain unease, as if they were escaped mental patients.

John watched this for about half an hour. The two of them were oblivious to John and everything else around them. At one point they spent five minutes studying a rubber band. John was pretty sure that wherever these guys were from rubber bands were a common item. He thought that this was a good enough time to check in on Barbara. When John went to Barbara's desk, she wasn't there. He walked around to Albert's desk. "Have you seen Barbara?" he asked Albert. Albert was busy working on the video he took of Blowgun's speech and didn't hear John's question. "Albert?"

Albert turned quickly and was surprised by John being there. "Sorry, I didn't hear you. I've been working on trying to translate that speech. I've downloaded this app that listens to a foreign language and translates it into English. But I've played the speech three times now and it keeps coming up with the same thing."

John shrugged. "I guess that means it works?"

Albert laughed. "That is until you hear the translation. You have to listen to this." Albert held up his phone pointed at the speaker of his computer. He then hit play on the computer which started the video and the phone app announced the speech in a computerized female voice.

"It is a burnt potato day. The angry blender is far away. But we will keep our purple gun ready for the fight of the squirrels who try and drink my blood."

John looked confused. Albert was still laughing. He looked at John. "See what I mean. The technology is just not there yet. It's amazing that it can do what it does, but it still has a long way to go."

"What language is that?" John asked Albert.

Albert shrugged. "Not sure. The program on my phone thinks it's Bulgarian, but obviously it doesn't do a good job of translating. It must be some sort of eastern European dialect."

John looked at the two investors. They had a ream of blank copy paper opened and were taking one sheet out at a time to study them attentively and then were putting them into multiple different piles.

...

When John arrived home Barbara was already there working on her laptop sitting at the kitchen table. She closed the top of her computer before John could see what was on the screen. John walked over and gave her a hug and kissed her on her forehead. "I missed going home with you, did you take a cab?"

"No, I walked," she calmly responded.

John wasn't sure how much to push. He thought she may be in shock. "Are you upset with your father?"

Barbara thought for a second. "No, I'm not upset with him. In fact, I understand why he did it. It all makes sense to me now." John looked at her with a confused look in his face. She reached up and caressed his cheek. "I know you won't believe me but this will work out for the best."

"You're right, I don't believe you." John debated asking but decided to anyway. "What did you and your father talk about in his office? You went in angrier than I've ever seen you in my life and then a few minutes later you walked out as calm and relaxed as you usually are." John started to snicker. "You have to tell me what he said to calm you down; I know I'll need to use that skill someday."

Barbara looked up at John, her head slightly tilted with a soft smile on her face. "I can't just yet, but I promise you that I will. It's going to take a few days, but you just have to trust me."

John looked at her beautiful blue eyes and knew that he couldn't be angry with her. He sighed. He knew he wasn't going to get any information from her at this moment. "I trust you."

"Thank you." Barbara had a relieved look on her face. "I've already made dinner, help yourself. I'm not hungry right now."

John walked over to the stove where a casserole dish was sitting on one of the burners. He grabbed a fork and took a taste, it was delicious. "This is great. Say the funniest thing happened after you left. Albert played back Blowgun's speech and ran it through a voice translator app on his phone." John's back was to Barbara so he didn't see the sudden concerned look on her face. "You should have heard the translation that the phone came up with. It was hysterical. It talked about angry blenders and squirrels drinking his blood."

126

"John--"

"Oh, wait, I haven't told you the best part. The started to do an inventory of the office. But not of the equipment or computers, but of paper clips, pencils, thumb tacks and acted like they had never seen them before--"

"John--"

"And they opened a ream of printer paper and looked at every sheet studying it for something. A blank sheet. And then they put them into many different piles."

"John!" Barbara finally yelled.

John looked surprised. "What?"

"You're going to want to stay clear of these guys."

"Are they dangerous?" Barbara didn't say anything. John now looked concerned. "Well, are they?"

"I don't know. It's just a feeling I get from being around them. I don't know who they are and where they come from. But I don't think they are who they appear to be."

"I don't think anyone knows who they are, including themselves." Barbara didn't laugh at John's attempted joke. "Is this part of what you can't tell me right now?"

Barbara paused and it looked like she was trying to be careful with what she was going to say. "Just be careful around them. I'm sure they will be gone soon enough."

John looked directly at Barbara with a lighthearted expression on his face. "I thought you weren't supposed to keep secrets from one another when you are married?"

She gave back a devilish smile. "I've never heard that before. Was it in the wedding vows?"

John brought a bowl of food over to the kitchen table and sat down across from Barbara. She looked up over the top of her laptop and stared at John. "Aren't you going to watch TV?" John gave an indifferent shrug. "Isn't there a Lionel Barrymore film festival on tonight? You marked the calendar two months ago." John got a surprised look on his face, remembering that he had been looking forward to watching his favorite actor. He quickly picked up his dinner and raced over into the living room and turned on the television.

When John woke up he looked at the clock and saw that it was almost one in the morning. John looked over to the kitchen and saw that Barbara was still working on her computer. "Are you coming to bed?"

Barbara shook her head. "Soon." John noticed she looked really tired but was focused on whatever she was working on. John went to bed. About two hours later he rolled over and saw that she was in bed and sleeping. John felt satisfied that she was finally getting some sleep. He put his arm around her and gave her a squeeze. She snuggled into his arms and started to snore.

The next morning Barbara was sluggish getting ready for work. By the time they got into the car she dozed off. John wanted to wake her and ask what she was working on so late into the night but she looked like an angel sleeping. John then thought do angels sleep? He wasn't paying attention and nearly went through a red light and slammed on the brakes. He looked over at Barbara, it didn't wake her. He looked back out his windshield. In the middle of the intersection Fred was standing there attempting to bite into an aluminum can. John carefully drove around Fred and up the street to the office. As soon as he pulled into the parking lot Barbara woke up as if an alarm clock had gone off. She looked awake, focused and ready to go.

When they walked in to the office John turned to

Barbara. "Get you a cup of coffee?" Barbara nodded. "The usual?" She nodded again. John looked over his shoulder as he walked to the break room and noticed that Barbara sat down, pulled a note pad and pencil out of her desk and sat there as if she was a student waiting for the professor to start a lecture.

John was pouring a cup of coffee when he noticed something different on the break room wall. The EEOC poster had been replaced. One side was written in a foreign language, something Russian looking. The other side was in Spanish. John brought out coffee for Barbara who was now feverishly taking down shorthand notes. John didn't realize that she knew shorthand but it made sense since she is the office manager. He put the coffee down in front of her. She looked up and mouthed thank you without making a sound and then went back to writing. John heard Blowgun and Zipper talking in their office. He wondered if Barbara was listening to them and taking notes. She looked up at him and waved her hands as if she was shooing him away from her desk.

John walked into the technician area. William was there looking up something on his computer. On the walls were handwritten banners in that same language in the break room. Looking at the signs he spoke to William. "What is this? What do they say?"

William looked up from his computer. "It's Bulgarian. Actually to be accurate it's the Cyrillic alphabet. It was invented in the tenth century by followers of St. Cyril who was a Greek missionary who basically invented a written language for them."

John felt relieved to at least now know what language he was looking at. "But what does it say?"

"Well, that's where it gets interesting. I figured out how to change my keyboard to mimic the Bulgarian alphabet and then typed the letters into an online translation website. In fact I changed Tim's keyboard to now type only in Bulgarian.

As if almost on cue, Tim came running into the technician area looking frantic. "Guys, you have to help me. My computer is broken. When I type on the keyboard it comes up as these crazy letters. Nothing matches the keyboard."

William did his best to keep from laughing. "New policy from the owners, Tim. They won't have the time to learn English so we are all going to have to learn Bulgarian. Isn't that right, John?"

John was not going to miss out on an opportunity to give Tim a hard time. "That's right Tim. We're all going to have to learn Bulgarian."

Tim got a panicked look on his face. "Oh, I can't do that. I can't." He turned to John and had a look of desperation. "John, you have to talk to them. Talk to Zipper, he seems to know some English."

John was holding his breath trying to keep from laughing. "I'll see what I can do, Tim." Tim had a panicked look on his face as he kept looking at John and William. He then suddenly went back to his office.

Anyway," William continued from where he left off, "I decided to translate what Zipper wrote up."

"How do you know it was Zipper?" John asked.

"Because he had ink all over his hands and most of his face. He tried to wash it off but didn't do a very good job of it. So that one over there says 'The Right Shoe Goes Better With Butter'. The one behind me says 'The Angry Blender Breaks His Pencil'. And the one above your head says 'Taste The Purple'."

John was very confused. "What does it mean?"

William shrugged. "Must be something lost in translation." He looked at the sign above John's head and developed a more serious look on his face. "But I doubt that the website would get it so mixed up."

"The same thing happened yesterday when Albert played Blowgun's speech into a translation app on his phone. It was just as bizarre as what is written here."

"Maybe it was Tim who gave them the expressions. You know how he gets things mixed up when he tries to give motivational speeches."

John shook his head slowly. "No, this is different. Tim is just an idiot. This is a much more serious level of craziness. This is what an insane person would say." John all of a sudden remembered what Barbara said to him last night about staying clear of the investors. He wondered if she knew more than she was letting on.

William turned to John pointing his thumb over his shoulder. "Well, it looks like one of the crazies is here right now." Zipper came into the room, saw that John and William were in there and got excited. He put out his hands with both palms out like he was signaling for them to stop or not move. John noticed that Zipper's hands were smeared with faded ink. "Shampoo!" he yelled and started to clap his hands. He then turned and ran out or the room.

William looked at John. "Guess he wants us to stay here. Or for us to wash our hair." Zipper came back a few seconds later ushering everyone else into the technician's room. Then he ran back out. Ten seconds later he came running in again holding a stack of blank pages and proceeded to slip. The paper flew up in the air and landed all over the room. Zipper shrieked and tried to catch the paper as it was falling. He stood looking at the blank paper lying on the ground with a disappointed look on his face. Blowgun walked into the room and had a disappointed look on his face, too. He patted Zipper on the shoulder and said something that no one understood but must have been comforting since

Zipper got happy again immediately.

Blowgun was no longer dressed as a seventeenth century noble. Today he was dressed as a prohibition era gangster in a pinstriped suit that still was way too small on him. He looked like he was ready to give another speech. Zipper stepped forward. "Hair loss Ford truck call now."

John realized that Zipper must have picked up English phrases from watching television commercials. He held up his hands and made a time out signal with his hands. Zipper looked at him confused and then mimicked what John did. John then held out his hands the same way Zipper did a few minutes ago. This Zipper understood and was very happy to feel like he was making a connection with John. Zipper looked at Blowgun who gave him a nod of approval. John looked around the room to see who could help him with an experiment. William was sitting there on the verge of a laughing fit. Tim was attentively listening to Zipper and looked like he was trying to contemplate what he said. Fred was over in the corner looking terrified. John had never seen him like that before. The new owners scared Fred for some reason. John actually understood why Fred felt that way. Barbara was giving John a stern look wondering what he was up to. John thought that he will have to skip using her in his experiment. His last hope was Albert who was watching this with keen interest.

"Albert, I want to try an experiment." John noticed that Barbara shot him a nasty glance. He looked at her. "I didn't forget. I just want to test something." She didn't change her glance. He looked back at Albert. "I want to test something, are you with me?"

Albert had an intrigued look on his face. "Sure, I'm with you. What do you got in mind?"

"I want to test that they don't know English. This will help us if we need to speak freely. You're an aspiring actor. You ready to take some direction?"

Albert smiled and put a hand up to his face. "I'm ready for my close up, Mr. DeMille."

"Ok Norma, I know it's that the pictures that got small. What I need for you to do is to appear very happy but insult Blowgun. You think you can do that?"

Albert put on a big grin. "You are the dumbest, fattest oaf I've ever seen. You look like a moron." Blowgun's eyes lit up and he had a big smile on his face. He grabbed Zipper's arm and shook it with excitement.

John was watching this very closely. "Ok, now say something polite but have a disappointed look on your face."

Albert now changed his expression to one of sad disappointment. "I think you are the greatest person in the world." Blowgun's face changed instantly watching Albert's expression.

John was now convinced that they didn't understand English but were just following their facial expressions. "Quick, before he thinks something is wrong smile and say anything."

Albert got a big smile on his face and looked Blowgun right in the eyes. "So this means we can say whatever we want as long as we don't arouse suspicion."

"Exactly." John was watching how Blowgun and Zipper were reacting and at the moment they looked pleased. "I think he wants to make another speech. Record it again just like yesterday."

"Should I turn on the translator app?" Albert asked.

John shook his head up and down smiling looking at Blowgun. "No, don't do that. Whatever you do, don't turn that back on. It could accidentally translate what we are saying into Bulgarian."

Albert nodded. "Good idea. Guess that's why you're the boss. Just started recording."

John looked at Zipper and shook his head up and down and gave him the thumbs up signal. John was hoping that maybe he caught a rerun of *Happy Days* and would understand. Zipper also gave a thumbs up to John. Blowgun patted Zipper on the shoulder and signaled for him to step aside which he promptly did. Blowgun then took a deep breath and began to speak.

John looked over at Barbara. He knew she was probably more worried than angry at him for playing this game. But he needed to know himself what he was dealing with and wanted to reaffirm his role as vice president. Blowgun got very animated during his speech. He kept saying the word burkachka often during his speech or usually would say yadosan burkachka. John wondered what that meant. He looked around the room and saw that Barbara was trying not to laugh. John wasn't sure if that was due to Blowgun looking ridiculous or if she understood what he was saying. The only other person who had any emotion was Fred who becoming more visibly frightened like a trapped animal fearful of its death. Fred would be the last person John would take seriously, but what if he had some sort of a sixth sense. John paid attention to Blowgun who was now crying and shaking his fists in the air as if he was yelling at god, then paused and put his hand over his heart as if he was saying a pledge.

After about ten seconds of silence, it appeared that Blowgun was finished. Zipper started to applaud. "We better applaud as well," John suggested to everyone else. They gave Blowgun a round of applause and he started to blow kisses to everyone and clasped his hands and then walked out of the room. He kept walking to the front door and walked out of the building. John looked at Albert. "Did you get that?"

Albert nodded. "Sure did boss."

Barbara looked over at John. "I'm going to need to talk to Zipper in private. You boys run off and have fun translating the speech." She had a slight grin on her face.

John looked concerned. "Do you think that's safe?"

Barbara smiled. "Of course, it's safe. The big one is off somewhere and Zipper here seems to be a gentleman. Right, Zipper?" Barbara looked at Zipper and gave him the thumbs up sign.

Zipper looked at Barbara with a big smile and put his thumbs up as well. "Diet Pepsi."

Barbara continued. "And I have nothing to worry about, I've got at least fifty pounds on him." She winked at John. She looked at Zipper and pointed to his office, he nodded and walked in front of her into the office and she followed behind and closed the door. John walked over to Albert's desk where he had setup the video on his computer and was getting ready for the translation app to load. He turned and looked at John. "We are ready." John nodded. William and Tim came over to listen as well. The video started and the phone spoke in its cold female mechanical voice.

"When my great, great, great uncle became octopus he know that the angry blender would one day be our great enemy. The blender know where you sleep. Blender will burn the mud. When the blender is angry he will be as big as the goat tree. The angry blender will break his pencil. We must use great purple ray gun and we defeat the blender. I have fought angry blender my life all. Zhelyazko has see angry blender and he use sharpened purple crayon and keep the blender away. We are here now and keep you all safe from blender. We buy company to sell electricity and we are far from the angry blender is why we know that magic potato will come from sky. And I yell at magic potato in sky you go back to angry blender and you say Blagun Kudline has purple ray gun and angry blender will taste the purple. And I swear on grave of uncle octopus no more angry blender find me and will stay angry in homeland over water."

They all stood quietly trying to absorb what they had just heard. William was the first to comment. "Yep, they're nuts," he muttered.

Albert sat back in his chair. "Guess my app is working properly after all." He let out a light chuckle. The phone then translated what Albert said into Bulgarian. A second later they heard someone behind them speaking Bulgarian that came across the phone translated. "That speak language good." They all turned and saw that Blowgun was standing there watching them and must have for some time.

John wanted to panic but thought that no one had said anything to tip Blowgun off. He also looked very happy and John thought that was a good sign he hadn't figured out what they were doing. "We were listening to your wonderful speech again." Albert's phone translated what John said.

Blowgun's eyes lit up with happiness. He started to talk and the phone translated. "This reminds of old proverb. Sailor one day walk on street down and he come up on talking pineapple. Pineapple say 'I give you wishes of three'. Sailor bites pineapple and many years later he open store of selling meat of horse."

They all stood there silent and paralyzed with fear. After a few moments of uncomfortable silence, John spoke. "Albert, you don't want your batteries to run down, you should turn that off." Albert quickly stopped the application. Blowgun nodded in agreement and said something. John took this as a sign of agreement. "Looks like saving battery use is a universal premise. Since we're safe again we need to make sure we keep looking happy in front of him." Blowgun responded with something that no one understood and then walked away.

"So, what are we to do if this angry blender finds us?" Tim asked with fear in his voice. "I don't have a purple ray gun."

William lived for moments like these and wasn't going to let this one slip away. "I don't know Tim; I think you are in serious danger. Better keep a look out for magic potatoes in the sky."

Tim was becoming more visibly frightened. "I haven't seen any magic potatoes. But I don't know what they look like."

"Look Tim, normally I would make fun of you for something like this, but you look really scared." William paused. "I know someone who sells purple ray guns."

Tim's eyes were filled with hope. "You do? How do you know these people? Can I buy one?"

"Let's just say I know people. But they cost about a hundred dollars."

Tim reached into his pocket and pulled out all of his cash and quickly counted it. "All I have is sixty two dollars." He handed it to William.

William grabbed the money from Tim's hands, folded it and put it in his pocket. "All right, I'll see what I can do. He owes me a favor. Your best bet is to go hide in your office until I come back." Tim shook his head in agreement and ran off to his office and slammed the door.

John looked at William. "You know it's not nice to take advantage of the stupid. I think this falls under bad karma."

William smiled. "Don't worry. I'm going to use the money for a good purpose. I'm going to the mall to buy a blender. I figure if I put that on his desk it will send him over the edge." William walked out of the office whistling a happy tune.

Barbara and Zipper walked out of Henry's old office. Zipper had a very pleased look on his face. "Do you remember Bert Fergurenson from Austin, Texas?" Barbara asked John nodding her head up and down.

John took Barbara's cue. "Of course, I remember Bert Fugleson. How is that old guy?"

"He's great. So as our new director of sales you will have to go visit him tomorrow. I'll get you on the red eye to Austin."

"Director of sales? Austin Texas?"

Zipper burst out with excitement. "Austin, Texas." He then made a gesture pretending to throw a football. "Red Sox."

John looked at Zipper and nodded his head slowly. "Yes, Red Sox." He then looked back at Barbara. "I'm not a salesman. Why am I going?"

"Because this is stuff my father used to take care of. And these two don't speak English. I will take care of it. Remember, trust me."

Zipper walked back to his office. John walked over to Barbara "What is going on?"

She gave him a kiss on the cheek. "I'll explain tonight. I need for you to pack up your desk. While you're gone I am going to move Tim out of his office and get you moved in." John shot Barbara a surprised look. "I'll take care of it."

"Ok, thanks. Do you want to get some lunch?"

"Can't today, I'm going to take Albert to lunch. I have something I need to go over with him and don't want to do it in the office. When you finish up with your desk, head on home and pack for the trip. I'll get the tickets this afternoon and bring them home with me." John nodded. "Thanks. Why don't you take a nap, I'll wake you when I get home."

John walked over to his desk and started to clean it out. Something just wasn't clicking. Who are these insane investors running the company? Why is Barbara making up customers and having him leave town? What is he going to do in Austin? John looked up and saw Albert grab a box and walk back to his desk. John got up to observe what he was going to do. Albert filled the box with a bunch of office supplies and personal items and then walked out to his car. Barbara came up behind John; he turned and saw her looking at him disapprovingly. "Did you just fire Albert?" John asked her.

"No, I did not." Barbara coldly replied.

John didn't believe her. "Then why is he packing up his desk?"

Barbara was beginning to lose her patience. "John, please go home. I promise you I will explain tonight." He gave her a doubtful look. "I will. I promise." She gave him a kiss and then walked outside and got into Albert's car.

John stood at the door and watched them drive off. He was starting to get worried. John turned around to go back to his desk but was shocked to see Fred standing right in front of him. Fred had a look of panic on his face. He grabbed John's shirt. "They are evil. You need to run. Don't come back." John gently pulled Fred's hands off his shirt. He nodded his head and turned from Fred and walked out to the parking lot and got into his car.

As he drove home John wondered why Fred did that and why did he actually understand his warning. John was getting scared; he felt that this is too much chaos for him to deal with. While he was waiting at the traffic light he looked out of the driver's side window and saw Death To Mimes spray painted on a wall. The light changed but John was mesmerized by this and kept staring at the wall. The car behind him honked. John was woken from his stupor and drove off. When he got home he laid down on the couch to try and think about what was going on. The next thing he noticed was Barbara walking in the front door and he realize that he had fallen asleep.

"I'm glad you got some sleep. You need it." Barbara sat down on the couch next to John to give him a hug.

John felt fuzzy and rubbed his eyes. "What time is it?"

"A little after seven."

"After seven? Why are you so late? What's the deal with Albert?"

Barbara sighed. "I'll tell you on the way to the airport. Your flight is at eleven. I need to get some sleep before I drive you over. Please wake me at nine-thirty. Have you packed yet?"

"No, not yet. I came home and lay down on the couch and I guess I just passed out."

"Pack lightly. Just take a carry on bag with you."

"How long will I be there? Barbara? Barbara?" Barbara had lain down and fallen fast asleep. John went into the bedroom and started to pack enough for two days. He came out of the bedroom, walked over to the bookcase and looked for a book to take with him.

"Honey, where is my copy of The *Fountainhead*?"

Barbara stirred. "I don't know. Take another book."

"I really don't want to read something else. I like reading that when I fly."

"Haven't you read it twice?"

"Well, it's been three times. I have a copy in my

140

desk. I can run over to the office and grab my copy."

"No, don't do that. I'll buy you one at the airport bookst..." Barbara drifted back to sleep.

John decided that he would have enough time to drive over to the office, grab the book and head back in time. He quietly left the apartment to let Barbara sleep.

When John arrived at work, he saw that the lights were on. He walked up to the front door and it was unlocked. He wondered if Blowgun and Zipper were still in there counting paper clips. John walked into the technician room and saw William was in there with a five gallon gas container and was tearing up a bed sheet. "What in the world are you doing?"

"I'm trying to set fire to the office." William calmly answered. "Why, what does it look like I'm doing?"

John was surprised at how honestly William answered him. "It looks like you're trying to set the office on fire."

"Then why did you ask?"

"I don't know?"

"What are you doing here?"

John was confused and was trying to understand the situation. "I came to get my copy of *The Fountainhead* before my flight."

"Oh, well you better get it before it burns. I heard it's a great novel. Where are you flying to?"

"Austin." John walked over to his desk and pulled out the book form the bottom drawer.

"Can I ask you why you are setting the office on fire?"

"Isn't it obvious?"

"Well, no it isn't?"

"Sorry, I should have said that differently. If you look at the situation, it's very obvious."

John was trying to understand what William was

taking about. "What's obvious about burning down the office? Furthermore, why are you setting the office..." John stopped in the middle of his sentence because it became clear to him. "The police, they were looking for you. You set your uncle's factory on fire."

"Well, to be honest, it wasn't my uncle's factory. I don't have an uncle."

"But you set fire to the factory?"

"Oh yeah, it was a nice burn. I went back a few days later. I was rather proud of my work. One of my best."

"So you're a pyromaniac?"

"No, a pyromaniac works for free. I'm a freelance arsonist."

"You're kidding me right? This is your profession? What, do you have business cards?"

William reached into his pocket, pulled out his wallet and plucked out a business card. He handed it to John. John looked at the card. It said William Argi Freelance Arsonist and underneath in italic letters *Professional Service* and listed his cell phone number. John went to hand the card back to William. "No, you keep that. You never know." John numbly put the card in his pocket.

"So you get paid to set fires?"

"Yes I do. In fact I get paid rather well. And it's tax free."

"Then it was you who was setting fire to your girlfriend's cats. And the front door of the office. You got paid for that?"

"No, I didn't get paid for the cats. I just hate cats. And it is pretty cool to watch them run around when they had been set on fire. The front door, that wasn't me. Those Brazilians are real sloppy." John was thinking why was the Brazilian mafia targeting the office and was just about to ask, but William stopped John before he could talk. "So why are you going to

Austin?"

John was trying to sort this out. "To be honest, I don't know anymore."

William looked John directly in the eyes with a serious look. "Go to Austin and don't come back. Take your wife with you. It's over John."

John was at a loss or words. First Barbara, then Fred, now William. Why is everyone trying to get him to leave. "How is it over?" John wanted to say more but he couldn't find the right words.

"Look John, the company is dead. Henry is gone. The new owners are insane. How long until one of them pulls a knife on someone or shoots up the place? Take it from a fellow criminal, these guys are no good. I would know. I'm sure there is some prison in Europe doing a bed count and coming up two short. Zipper raced out of here this afternoon after he was with Barbara and hasn't been seen since. Albert is already gone. Fred is terrified of them. Fred of all people. I've seen that guy stand in the middle of the road with cars flying by him and he wouldn't flinch. Now he cowers in the corner. And Tim," William put a blender on the desk in front of him, "he won't be seen for a long time. John looked at the blender. It had a face drawn on it with the eyebrows curved down, a frown where a mouth would be. On its sides were two pipe cleaners taped to the blender that were shaped as arms. One of the arms had a broken pencil taped to it.

John was in shock as if he had been dumped into a pool of ice cold water. He was now awake. He now understood. The company is dead. But did it need to be burned to the ground? "But why burn it?"

"In India when the soul has left the body you burn the empty shell. The soul has left the building. It is time to burn it."

John stood there silent for about a minute. William just stared at John waiting to see what he was going to do. "You're right, the company is dead. It needs to be burned. But who hired you to burn the building?"

"I think you need to talk to your wife." At that moment William's phone rang. John was confused why William would tell him to talk to his wife. William answered his phone. "Yeah, yeah, he's right here. Yes, he is." William put his phone down and looked at John. "I think you need to talk to your wife."

"I got you the first time. I'll go home and talk to my wife."

"No, I think you need to talk to your wife." William handed his phone over to John.

John carefully took the phone from William. He slowly put it up to his year. "Hello?"

Barbara was on the other end. "John, come home."

"It's ok, honey, I now know what is going on and I am ok with it."

"John, I need for you to come home now."

"I don't think you understand. I agree with burning the building down."

"John, come home now. Hand the phone back to William."

John handed the phone back to William. William put it to his ear. "Yeah, I see, ok." He then hung up the phone and started to pack up his equipment.

John looked confused. "Is that it? You're not going to set the building on fire?"

"Nope, it's been called off. Postponed to a later date." William got all of his items and was ready to walk out. John stood there motionless. "John, go home to your wife and don't come back here again." John slowly nodded. "Oh, and don't forget your book." John picked up his book and followed William out of the building. He got into his car and drove home.

John parked his car in front of the apartment building and sat there for a minute debating whether or not he should go in. After everything that has happened over the past two days John wasn't sure how much more of this he can take. He stared out of the front windshield looking at the apartment building and remembered when he dropped off Barbara after their first date. He was hoping to see her turn on the lights in her apartment. As it turns out her apartment faced the back of the building so it couldn't be seen from the street. Yet John was concerned why his wife was keeping secrets from him. He knew he loved her and didn't want to leave her. Also he thought, how far could he get? To leave you need to plan out where you are going, have enough money, even change your identity. John got out of the car and went into the apartment building.

When he walked into the apartment Barbara dropped a handful of papers she was holding onto the kitchen table and ran to John and hugged him. "Why did you go back to the office? I was so scared. What if you got there ten minutes later? I don't want to live without you." John noticed that she was crying, something he had never seen before. He caressed her hair and held her tight. After a minute Barbara stopped crying and looked at John. "I'm sorry. When I woke up and didn't see you here I was scared that you could have been injured in the fire."

"Why didn't William set fire to the office tonight?"

"Because the genius set off the alarm. I was awakened when the alarm company called me. I called him and told him to stop. The last thing we need is for the police to have evidence. Such an idiot and his business card claims he's a professional."

"Look, I need to know what is going on right now."

Barbara sighed. "I know. I will tell you everything on

the way to the airport. Grab your bag. Do you have your book?"

John forgot all about the book. "The book?" He thought for a second. "Right, I left the book in the car." Barbara nodded and went over to the kitchen table and gathered up all of the papers and put them into a manila envelope. She then reached down and picked up a small suitcase. John looked surprised. "Where are you going?"

"I'm going to meet you there, but I'm driving. I have to make a few stops along the way. Are you ready? Let's go now."

While they were driving John waited a few minutes before he said anything. "So are you going to tell me what is going on?"

Barbara sighed. "I will but I need to do something first." She picked up her phone and dialed a number.

"Who are you calling?"

"Hold on, I need to leave a message." John noticed that Barbara was nodding along as if she was listening to someone talking. She then spoke in a deep raspy voice that was very menacing. "Burkachka znae kak da pluva." She then hung up and put her phone down.

"What was that? What did you say? It sounded almost like something Blowgun would say." Barbara didn't say anything; she just stared forward out towards the road. "Hello, are you there? What is going on?"

Barbara waited a few seconds as if she was collecting her thoughts. "Blowgun and Zipper are two escaped mental patients from an insane asylum in Sofia, Bulgaria." John was shocked and partially satisfied since that is what he thought they were. "Blowgun is a descendant of an old royal family from the twelfth century. He has been in the institution

146

since he was a small child. He is incredibly paranoid. He believes that there is a giant angry blender that has been chasing him his entire life. He thinks that if he is not in Europe the blender can't find him. And if it does, he is safe because he doesn't think that blenders can swim. He believes if he can build the perfect ray gun that can shoot purple, he can defeat the blender."

"So how did he buy the company?"

"His family is incredibly wealthy. After the fall of communism all of the family assets were unfrozen allowing him access to the money. He bribed his way out of the asylum for himself and Zipper. He bought the company from my dad since he thought he could find the parts he needs to build the ray gun."

John had so many questions running through his head. But he knew he couldn't ask them all at once. He decided to start with the basic foundation questions. "So how does Zipper come into the picture? Is he scared of the blender too?"

"Yes and no. He claimed that he has seen the blender before and so he supports Blowgun in his attempts to defeat the blender. But he has no fear of the blender. He ended up in the asylum when he was a child. He's from a small town in southern Bulgaria; I think it was Oreshnik he said. When he was five he sharpened crayons into a sharp weapon and stabbed all the students in his kindergarten class, most of them in the neck. Seven children died."

"Why did he do it?"

"He said that it was because he couldn't tell the difference between the orange yellow and the yellow orange crayon. He said that he doesn't regret killing the children but is still bothered by the crayons. I told him he needs to go to Death Valley since it is so hot there crayons will melt."

"So that would explain why William saw him running from the office. Wait a second, how did you tell this to him?"

"That's what I was doing last night. I learned enough Bulgarian to communicate with them." John then remembered back to their first date when Barbara spoke to the waiter in Norwegian and she told him that she can learn a language very quickly.

John stared out the front windshield and wondered what he done in his life to get him to this point. He felt like he was going to have a panic attack. The first thing to pop into his mind was being at his mother's funeral and watching his father cry. His relatives were fighting with one another and for the first time felt the fear that he will die one day. Until he started dating Barbara, John always thought he was going to be alone. When he married her he knew that he had someone who he could always trust, someone who will always take care of him, someone who was his partner. Someone he could have at his side as he fought the universe. With her he is no longer alone. With her he finally felt safe; she was the antithesis of anarchy. But now he felt his world falling apart.

"Take this envelope." Barbara handed John the manila envelope. "This has everything you will need when you land. Make sure you take out your passport before you get on the plane."

John laughed. "My passport? Since when do I need a passport to go to Texas?"

"You're not going to Texas. You're flying into Vancouver."

John's jaw dropped. "What?" John was struggling for words. "Canada?" He felt dizzy and nauseous. "Are you kidding?"

Barbara was silent for a moment. "No, I am not kidding. You need to read what is in that envelope when you are on the plane. Don't let anyone see you reading it. Now listen to me, you need to follow everything to the letter. Do you understand? John?" John slowly nodded, unable to say anything surprised to see Barbara shouting at him. "We're going to have to leave the country for good."

"Want to tell me what's going on?" John was beginning to get very nervous. "Why are we fleeing the country?"

Barbara took in a deep breath and let it out. "Because I embezzled every last cent from the company." John turned and looked at Barbara and didn't say anything. He waited for her to continue. "I make sure all necessary outstanding bills were paid and tied up some loose ends. The rest I then turned to cash."

John turned his head to look out the passenger side window. He was at a loss for words. He felt like he was in a bad dream that wouldn't end. "What's going to happen to everyone else at work?"

"I gave Albert a nice severance package. He has enough funding to make part two and three of his trilogy. William got paid to take care of the building which should be taken care of by tonight. I don't know about Tim and to be honest I really don't care. And Fred is well taken care of; he hasn't had to work for years now. He's set for life"

John's feeling of panic subsided at the opportunity to finally find out about Fred. "All right I have to know. What is the deal with Fred?"

"Fred is the reason why Jenkins Electrical is actually a company." John looked at Barbara with a raised eyebrow. He could not believe what he heard. "No, it's true. The guy is a genius. IQ of one hundred and eighty. He has a PhD in physics."

"So why does he eat garbage? Why does he sleep

on the streets?"

"Who knows? Maybe he took too much LSD? Or he has serious mental issues? This much I know. When dad bought the factory, Fred was squatting in the warehouse area. Dad got his hands on some electrical equipment that didn't work very well. Fred took it apart and put it back together again working. Dad hired him to be the company technician and he would go out and sell the equipment cheap and make it up with a lifetime repair warranty. Fred would go out and fix these things until they would break again. Every new piece of equipment that dad would buy he would figure out right away how it worked and would become an expert on it."

John thought that made sense. He remembered that while working with Fred was not the easiest thing to do, but he did know everything about every piece of equipment. "So why is he set for life?"

"Back in those days my mom did the payroll. She noticed that Fred was not cashing his paychecks. So she opened a bank account for him and got him a place to live. Since he lives very frugally, he spends very little money. After almost thirty years that builds up. Probably millions by now. After my mom passed away, dad hired an attorney to manage the money and make sure that Fred always was taken care of."

"So was he always so weird?"

"Not always. I remember as a little girl sometimes I would be at the office and he was normal and then other days he seemed catatonic like he was a zombie. After mom died he got much worse. She seemed to be the only one who would look out for him and he took her death very hard."

"You still haven't told me why we have to leave the country. What am I going to do in Canada?"

"My father will take care of everything." John shot a

surprised look at Barbara. "He has a farm in Manitoba that we can stay at that grows papayas."

John started to laugh. "Aren't papayas grown in tropical climates? How can you grow them in Canada?"

"You can if the ground is radioactive." Barbara calmly replied. John was taking a sip from a water bottle and proceeded to choke and spit out the water coughing violently. Barbara reached over to gently pat his back and put her hand on his cheek. "I'm probably telling you too much right now; it will all make sense real soon."

"I though you weren't talking to your father?" Barbara looked like she wanted to say something but held back. "What happened in your father's office yesterday? You walked in with a look like you were going to kill him and when came out you were calm."

"I guess I should tell you what happened. But I want you to know that I love you and want to be with you for the rest of our lives. I know that the past two days have been crazy, but I promise you that I will make it right. Things will calm down and I want you to be there with me."

John was getting annoyed. "What happened?"

"All right, I'll tell you."

Henry walked into his office and Barbara followed behind him slamming the door behind her. She stood staring angrily at Henry with her arms folded. "You have to listen to me kid," Henry pleaded, "I had no choice." Barbara didn't change her posture. "The Brazilian mafia was after me and I had to get them money. It's not like I can go to the bank and ask for a business loan to pay off the mafia."

Barbara unfolded her arms but still was visibly angry. "So who are those rubes?"

"I found them at the train station. They were going

through the garbage collecting anything purple and putting it into a pile."

"Why in the world would you go near them?"

"I don't know why. But I did. When I approached them I saw that they had a duffel bag full of cash. The short one turned to me and started babbling something I couldn't understand and then said, "Purple ray gun." I told him I can get him a purple ray gun. They got in the car with me and when I got to the building I held up the keys and pointed to the building. Then I pointed to the duffel bag. They talked amongst themselves and seemed to agree. I handed them the keys and they handed me the bag."

Barbara was no longer angry. "What do we do now? This isn't like your other deals in the past. Those could be covered up with creative bookkeeping. But this here is different."

"I was trying to fix the whole eel thing with the new equipment, but the Brazilians were not willing to wait."

"So do we dupe these guys and take back the company?"

"No kid, this is too far gone. I'm going to pay off the mob and we need to split town. Liquidate the rest of the company and we'll cross the border."

"Should I call Lou Corticidin?"

"Can't, he died a few years ago."

Barbara started to laugh. "Don't tell me he finally got up the nerve to kill himself?"

"Kind of. I talked to his kid about a year ago. He was going to jump of an eight story building. While he was going up on the fire escape he slipped on the seventh floor and fell to his death. But his son still is in the same business."

"I'll get in touch with him. He'll need to get new identities for you, me and John." Henry looked at Barbara with a questioning look. "I am not leaving without my husband."

Henry nodded. "Fine. But he can't know what's going on. He's a good kid but a bit too honest. I can't risk him screwing things up."

Barbara shook her head in agreement. "Ok, I will take care of him. Where will we meet?"

"Head towards that farm in Manitoba. Send your husband to Vancouver to get his stuff at that PO Box near the airport. I'll get him a car and some money. Then have that idiot Walter burn down the office."

"Do you mean William?"

"Yeah, whatever that schmuck's name is. At least we won't regret not getting the insurance money when he's done. If he's not burning down the wrong building then he's leaving so much evidence behind proving that it was arson."

"Consider it done. What about the rest of the staff?"

"Who's that fruitcake you work with?"

"Albert."

"Pay him off. He's a good kid and he kept his mouth shut. Fred is covered by the trust fund. And Tom, see if he can be here in the building when it's burned to the ground."

Barbara smiled. "I'll see what I can do."

John felt numb. He didn't know what to say. He wasn't even sure if this was his wife. "So is William going to burn down the building?"

"It really doesn't matter at this point, but I'm sure he will." Barbara turned towards John and saw that he was leaning his head on the window with a depressed look on his face and was looking down at the ground. "I'm sorry I yelled at you before. You'll be fine. I couldn't tell you what I was doing until now. But I need for you to stay with me. Can you do that?" John didn't know what to do. He saw that they had arrived at the airport. Barbara pulled up to the airport departure zone. She gave John a hug and a long kiss. "I love you and I will see you soon."

John got out of the car and stood staring at Barbara. She looked back at him lovingly and smiled. "I just need to know one thing before you leave. What did you say to Blowgun?"

"I told him that blenders know how to swim."

John nodded slowly and then watched Barbara quickly drive away.

The End

Acknowledgments

There are many people that I would like to thank who helped me with this novel.

Thank you to Ms. Mother-In-Law for her exceptional editing since weakness is mine I have grammar with.

To my brother Paul who I consider the funniest person I know who also helped with the editing and I was honored to know that it made him laugh.

To my wonderful wife Christiana whom I am still scared will kill me if I don't thank her again.

To the Seattle Seahawks, the best team in the NFL. Go Hawks!

To all of my friends and family who supported me and offered ideas that I used in this story.

And to my amazing parents Terry and George who raised me with the values of hard work, honesty and unconditional love. It is because of them I have my sense of humor.

Made in the USA
Charleston, SC
03 September 2014